Beyond Cloud: Distributed Power

Alisha

Contents

Chapter 1

Introduction

Computing trend has experienced some back-and-forth switch between centralized and distributed controls. From mainframe computers which were mainly centralized, to distributed architectures such as personal computers (PCs), local networks and P2P systems. Cloud computing brought centralization with it, offering attractive advantages to business owners and their clients. But the sharp growth of connecting devices in number and capacity, has caused genuine doubts on the ability of cloud computing infrastructure to cope with the rising demands, in a way that satisfies the requirements of real time applications. As a result, decentralization once again has the baton [3], in order to accommodate the needs of IoT and related services.

Despite its many advantages, cloud computing suffers from issues related to latency, privacy and trust [3][4]. The number of connecting devices is estimated to hit 1 trillion by 2025 [5], and with such number and the massive amount of data they would be generating, relying on the remote cloud infrastructures for all computations may cause delay and bandwidth-related issues. Real-time applications may find it difficult to cope. To overcome these problems and provide better user experience for real-time and latency-sensitive applications, focus is now on distributed cloud technologies such as Cloudlet, Mobile Edge Computing (MEC), Fog computing and Mobile edge-clouds [6]. These and similar paradigms are under the edge computing concept, which has attracted huge attention recently due to its potential in addressing the inherent weaknesses associated with cloud computing.

The main idea behind the emerging edge computing technologies involves bringing data processing/computing and storage closer to the network edge, so that request and response time is considerably minimized. Each paradigm may have its primary target application and a slightly different approach, but the concept is usually similar. In some cases, a mini server is brought closer to the edge devices, so that some computation and storage tasks can be done and returned quickly without going through remote data centers, which would be the case in traditional cloud computing. In other cases, it is more distributed, with less need for mini servers. Mobile devices in close proximity simply pool their resources together, forming an easy to access "cloud" which functions in a P2P fashion.

Edge computing technologies are not meant to completely replace cloud computing, but are rather meant to work with it. Notwithstanding, they can also work independently. In particular, mobile edge-clouds can function independently with little or no infrastructural support. This makes it important for services in areas where there may be little or no traditional infrastructure, such as rescue operation scenarios in cases of emergency, improving user experience in crowded venues where infrastructure may be under strain, and searching for missing persons (e.g. children) in a crowded place. As a branch of P2P, these technologies inherit serious security concerns in addition to peculiar threats and attacks. Such attacks would mar the huge efforts that are currently being made in bringing edge computing to reality, and further truncate its benefits if unchecked.

In the literature, there are many reports which have highlighted some of the security concerns that are associated with distributed protocols. Many of these reports have proposed trust and reputation systems (TRSs) as viable for addressing the security concerns without incurring outrageous overhead.

TRSs have been applied to tackle different kinds of attacks in earlier P2P systems [7–13]. Successful online commercial services such as Ebay and Amazon use some of these methods to help users to discern who to transact with, based on their reputation. Kazaa also used a reputation management system, where users rate the participation level of each other, by giving more grade to those that share genuine contents frequently [8]. Similarly, BitTorrent adopts a 'give and take' method known as tit-for-tat. Although this is not exactly a reputation based system, it also rewards users that contribute more to the network.

We agree that TRS can be adapted to address security issues both in the old and emerging distributed networks. This work is therefore TRS-based, but it is focused on fully (or relatively more) distributed environments, including mobile edge-clouds. Emphasis is also on resource constrained devices who cannot afford resource intensive security protocols. We derive trust through reputation and familiarity concepts, as discussed in later chapters.

Nowadays, a discussion around distributed protocols/networks may seem incomplete if blockchain is not mentioned. In a nutshell, it is a distributed ledger which is shared among its users, allowing them to perform sensitive transactions without needing an intermediary or central authority. The ledger allows several parties in a network or system to add transactions, such that any change made consistently reflects across every copy. Because it is distributed, ledger reconciliation becomes easier, but it may attract some computational and storage cost. Many consider it a trustless system, but as we shall highlight, there is crucial need for trust. Infact, TRS has been proposed as a way to strengthen the blockchain system, so that it can overcome some known attacks.

Due to its vast application, we have explored the blockchain system, both as a distributed system that can benefit from TRS, and as a tool used to further solidify security in the proposed system. We propose a system that leverages its core attributes to secure our TRS system such that reputation scores would be shielded from badmouthing, slandering and other forms of attacks.

1.1 Motivation

The proposed system is based on reputation and trust. Trust has been identified as a crucial concept in digital security, without which it would be difficult to reason about the security of any system in a convincing manner [14]. In the absence of central entities that check and certify the activities of nodes in a network, each peer is left to fend for itself. Outside the digital world, people as social entities have the ability to discern whether or not to engage a neighbour in a given transaction. Sometimes people meet for the first time and get along well, and thus establish some kind of relationship. Other times their meeting may not lead to further transactions or cooperation.

Such ability to build relationships and transact without recommendation from certificate authorities or similar agencies is made possible for entities in digital platforms via TRSs. As mentioned previously, the literature contains many proposals on trust which are targeted at distributed networks, including P2P. But there are some lapses that need to be addressed to make TRSs fairer and more secure for the old and emerging distributed networking paradigms, including mobile edge-clouds. This is important because the relatively new technologies have peculiar security needs in addition to other loopholes which they inherit from their parent protocols. Some of the noted lapses include the following:

1. Most earlier methods focus mainly on how to mitigate attacks from malicious nodes after they have joined the network, but pay less attention to stopping or limiting malicious peers from joining initially. Those who attempt to overcome this limitation often require pre-established trust relationships over other channels, or some central entity such as server or super nodes which can constitute prime target for attacks. The new method overcomes these barriers and provides a distributed and fairer means of bootstrapping reputation scores for newcomers. This, by extension, makes it more suitable for mobile edge-clouds because the need for central entities or super nodes are eliminated, and nodes with low resources can participate easily.

2. Current methods tend to channel huge effort towards protecting client nodes from malicious server nodes (or seeders), but little attention is given to the protection of server nodes from malicious clients, especially in distributed P2P platforms. This gives rise to a form of bandwidth attack [15, 16] which has escaped the attention of nearly all TRSs in the literature. This attack has been shown to have adverse potential effect on security and fairness in distributed networks. To the best of our knowledge, our work is the first to tackle bandwidth attack (on seeders) in a distributed P2P reputation model, based on actual leecher-to-leecher behavior of peers. The new method empowers both client and server nodes to directly identify attackers and act fairly. This is important for many mobile edge-clouds use-cases, such as file sharing in crowded venues which was mentioned earlier.

3. It is a common practice to use interaction experiences between a "trustor" and a "trustee" to determine reputation and trust. In some cases, the number of good

interactions minus the bad ones normally form the bases for direct reputation and trust scores. Other times, it is based on the ratio of the good transactions to the total number of interactions. But the cumulative interaction rate barely reflects in the end result. This mostly leads to situations where more familiar node(s) may have little or no noticeable advantage over a less familiar one. Using the ratio method as an example, if node_A has 4 good interactions out of a total of 5, and node_B has 40 good interactions out of a total of 50, they may have the same score.

In the new method, the interaction rate concept (or 'familiarity') is accounted for, as a way of encouraging nodes to engage actively in the network. When it comes down to node_A and node_B, the proposed method leans towards node_B, while paying attention to how recent the bad scores are. If two nodes have similar reputation scores, the new method would give priority to the agent with higher interaction rate.

Each peer is monitored to see how much they have invested in the network relative to its capability and with respect to how much they have gained from network. This concept of familiarity is similar to the idea of personal trust, coined by Williamson [17]. It played a significant role towards mitigating bandwidth attacks in the proposed system.

4. The recommendation systems which is used to gather indirect trust information in most TRSs are prone to badmouthing and slandering attacks [18]. The trust score is only useful if the recommendation upon which they are based is sincere. Each recommendation giver is responsible for the recommendation it gives, while the receiver can only try to sieve the recommendations using some methods such as weighted average. But if many nodes lie about their recommendations, even such methods would not be effective. We involved the blockchain technology in the proposed method to address this problem. Unlike [18], our system does not just give a zero or one rating for downloaded files, and it is adapted for BitTorrent and similar other protocols. A lightweight consensus mechanism is proposed to make it usable for resource constrained devices.

1.2 Research Objectives

This research work is aimed at building on the literature to establish a more robust trust-based system for improving security and fairness among entities in distributed networks. This is done in a manner that makes peers able to reason autonomously, and make favorable security decisions even amidst several malicious parties. It will also be able to bootstrap trust efficiently to reflect actual behaviour of any newcomer, thereby encouraging consistent fairness within (and across) platforms, and discouraging maliciousness including free-riding, whitewashing, bad-mouthing, Sybil, collusion and fake-block attacks. These attacks shall be discussed in subsequent chapters. The sub tasks which will lead to the research goal include:

1. In-depth studies of existing security approaches (both trust based and otherwise) that are already in the literature for this kind of network, with the aim of identifying the best ones and building on them to establish a more efficient system that will function in the midst of higher percentage of maliciousness, and in a fully distributed platform.

2. Extracting and digitizing vital contexts, for peers' assessment. As part of this objective, effective methods have been derived to tackle the cold-start (or bootstrapping) problem [19] so that new peers can be fairly introduced into the network, instead of simply assigning initial positive scores to them, or using other non-optimal heuristics.

3. Applying suitable mathematical techniques to analyze, and grade the extracted contexts. This is important because if the extracted contexts are not properly correlated, they would make little or no meaning. We therefore apply adequate mathematical and statistical methods to capture the needed contexts.

4. Building a robust algorithm that will enable entities to assess their counterparts in order to make secure and fair decisions on communication issues such as allowing access to its resources or otherwise. The algorithm will be tested on simulated (and containerized) test-beds, which reflect the attributes of mobile edge-clouds, and some other popular distributed protocols.

5. A lightweight integration of the new system into blockchain is also proposed, so that participating nodes would reach a consensus concerning the reputation of

every peer. Trust scores are recorded immutably, and made easily accessible. With this feature, we further intend to make the system capable of featuring effectively in more than one kind of distributed platform, since a node's reputation can be used across similar network environments.

1.3 Contributions

Following the approved work plan for this book, our main contributions, some of which are already published, are summarized thus:

1. The literature of TRSs in popular distributed protocols such as P2P have been surveyed, highlighting their strengths and weaknesses. We identified popular weaknesses that need to be addressed in order to make the system stronger and more suitable for real-life application, especially on emerging edge computing systems.

2. We derived a novel method for bootstrapping reputation, so that the scores reflect the actual behaviour of new nodes, without placing existing nodes at disadvantage. A Sybil attacker may, for example, outsource puzzle computation, enabling it to maneuver the puzzle system of introducing new nodes, but our system is immune to this because it may be more difficult to outsource bandwidth. This will make more sense when we explain the bootstrapping method later.

3. We developed means of mitigating Bandwidth attack [15] which was neglected in the literature of TRSs. Our method allows seeders (service providers) to also be able to assess their clients in a distributed manner, based on first-hand information.

4. The system was tested on a simulated test-bed, which reflects the attributes of mobile edge-clouds; an edge computing paradigm that is considered potentially vital for IoT. Mobile edge-clouds can improve user experience among low-resource nodes, with little or no dependence on traditional communication infrastructures. The test-bed was also made to feature the attributes of older P2P platforms such as BitTorrent, since our approach is aimed at being applicable to the new paradigms as well as their parent protocols.

5. A version of the proposed method was adapted for IoT based eHealth system. We explained how mobile edge-clouds would function with fog nodes to bring about

improved Quality of Service (QoS), and service availability even in cases of natural disaster which would make fog nodes and other infrastructures unavailable. This would aid rescue operation and sustained eHealth services to people in the affected area.

6. We also propose the application of Blockchain technology to further secure trust/reputation scores for every peer, so that badmouthing and similar attacks would be very difficult or impossible. Knowing that we are focused on environments that may involve heavy presence of low resource mobile devices, a lightweight consensus mechanism was proposed.

1.4 Publications

So far, here are the publications that have been made with respect to this book:

1. Nwebonyi, F. N., Martins, R., & Correia, M. E. (2018, August). Reputation-Based Security System For Edge Computing. In Proceedings of the 13th International Conference on Availability, Reliability and Security (p. 39).

2. Nwebonyi, F. N., Martins, R., & Correia, M. E. (2019). Reputation based approach for improved fairness and robustness in P2P protocols. Peer-to-Peer Networking and Applications, 12(4), 951-968.

3. Nwebonyi, F. N., Martins, R., & Correia, M. E. (2019). Security and Fairness in IoT Based e-Health System: A Case Study of Mobile Edge-Clouds. In 2019 International Conference on Wireless and Mobile Computing, Networking and Communications (WiMob) (pp. 318-323). IEEE.

The literature review was documented in article number 2. This publication also contains the implementation and results of the proposed system in a P2P protocol. The system reflects to a large extent the general attributes of P2P.

Article number 1 has its emphasis on the attributes of mobile edge-clouds, as a case study for edge computing and IoT services. This was done by minimizing the functionality of the tracker to reflect, among other changes, the characteristics of the new protocol.

There were no significant difference in the results compared to the results of article number 2, mainly because the system was aimed at being as distributed as possible from the beginning.

The third paper focused on the application of mobile edge-clouds in IoT based eHealth systems, as well as the role of the proposed system in attaining inexpensive security in such distributed and volatile environment. This was done with full awareness of the sensitivity of information that potentially flow in such platforms. Results differ a little here, because some attributes of the proposed method were downplayed since they were considered non crucial for the eHealth setting.

1.5 book Structure

The remaining part of the book is organized as follows:

- Chapter 2 reports the concept of trust and reputation. It features popular definitions of trust, as well as how it is built and conceptualized. We report the meaning of reputation and various methods applied throughout the literature to compute them. In this chapter, we also discussed distributed networks and the prevalent attacks that they face. The advent of edge computing technology was equally reported here alongside its different paradigms, including fog computing, mobile edge computing (MEC), cloudlet, edge-centric computing, osmotic computing, and mobile edge-clouds.

- Chapter 3 discusses the literature review, bordering on TRSs and their application in various distributed platforms to mitigate attacks. Detailed discussion concerning its application on distributed networks, such as P2P, edge computing, blockchain technology and mobile adhoc networks (MANETs) were documented.

- Chapter 4 documents the proposed system, called FBit. It also reports experimental results obtained via simulations. Different attacks were simulated including Fake-block attack, Bandwidth attack, Sybil attack, and Collusion attack.

- Chapter 5: this chapter discusses the application of mobile edge-clouds for improved quality of service in IoT based eHealth system. It also discusses other use-cases of mobile edge-clouds including user-generated replay, rescue assistance in cases of emergency, and searching for missing persons in a crowd. In each case, the application of FBit for improved security is explained.

- Chapter 6 presents proposals for: (i) A version of the proposed system called FBit-U, which is aimed at testing the system in a containerised network setting, using docker and other tools. The goal is to attain a more realistic test environment since it would be super expensive to purchase hundreds of physical devices for the experiment. (ii) Adapting FBit-U into a blockchain system, so that trust scores would be publicly available and decision making would be more transparent. The system may significantly reduce or eliminate the chances of false recommendations: it is tagged Distributed Trust Ledger (DTL). This is not yet completed/tested.

- Chapter 7 presents the conclusion and outlines future work.

Chapter 2

The Concepts of Trust and Distributed Networks

As mentioned in the previous chapter, trust-based methods can be applied to secure distributed networks. Here, the actual meaning of trust is given, as well as how it is related to security, and why it is considered suitable for distributed networks. We shall define trust and related concepts, and establish its link to digital security. In addition, we shall discuss distributed networks, including P2P, edge computing and related protocols. By explaining them and their attributes, it would be easy to understand why trust is necessary for security in such platforms.

2.1 Meaning of Trust

Trust has almost become synonymous to security, it has been identified as a crucial concept in digital security; without which it would be difficult to reason about the security of any system in a convincing manner [14]. Trust can play a crucial role in making cooperation possible among different agents or groups. It is different from a feeling of affection or warmth, but involves a deliberate regulation of how much an agent is willing to depend on another.

The study of trust (and mistrust) in its empirical form kick-started in late 1950s, as a result of increased suspicion which the cold war created. By late 1960s, the study of trust took a more individual focus due to increased suspicion which people were having against their authorities and institutions: trust was conceptualized as a personality trait. Increase in divorce rate and other changes in (American) families is said to have motivated trust research in the 1980s, and it was geared towards interpersonal relationships. From 1990s till present, technological shifts and advancements have led to the study of trust as a solution to crucial economical, sociological and computational issues [20].

The application of formal and informal controls to motivate cooperation and thus trust, was proposed in 1990s: it allows trustworthy agents to reap some kind of benefits for acting reliably [21, 22]. This has since been applied in online systems such as Ebay and Amazon, and is being constantly explored for application in modern distributed platforms.

Despite its generally agreed importance, trust is difficult to define, mainly due to its complexity as a concept. Scholars have therefore defined it in a number of ways, but they all reflect a generally accepted behaviour of an agent in a community (i.e. reputation) in addition to other relevant concepts.

According to Tschannen-Moran and Hoy, "trust is one party's willingness to be vulnerable to another party based on the confidence that the latter party is benevolent, reliable, competent, honest and open" [20]. Gambetta et al. defines it as a level of subjective probability on which a party bases his assessment that another party will act in a certain manner, before monitoring the action (or even if he is not able to monitor it), and given that the assessment affects his own action [23]. Fukuyama defines trust as the expectation which arises in a community as a result of honest, regular and cooperative behaviour, as agreed by other members of the community based on mutual norms [24].

According to Cummings & Bromily, trust is the belief of an agent or group of agents that another party or group will (a) make sincere efforts to behave in compliance to any commitment; implicit or explicit, (b) is honest in any negotiation that precede such commitment, (c) does not take advantage of another in excessive manner, even if the opportunity exists [25]. And Mishra described trust as the willingness of one party to be vulnerable to another believing that the latter is competent, open, reliable and concerned [26].

To consider an entity trustworthy means to have high probability that such entity will act favorably or at least in a manner that is not harmful. Trust is context dependent, which is like saying that you can trust a lawyer's legal advice but not his advice on how to fix your car. It is usually based on some sort of relationship; direct, indirect or both as illustrated in figure 2.1.

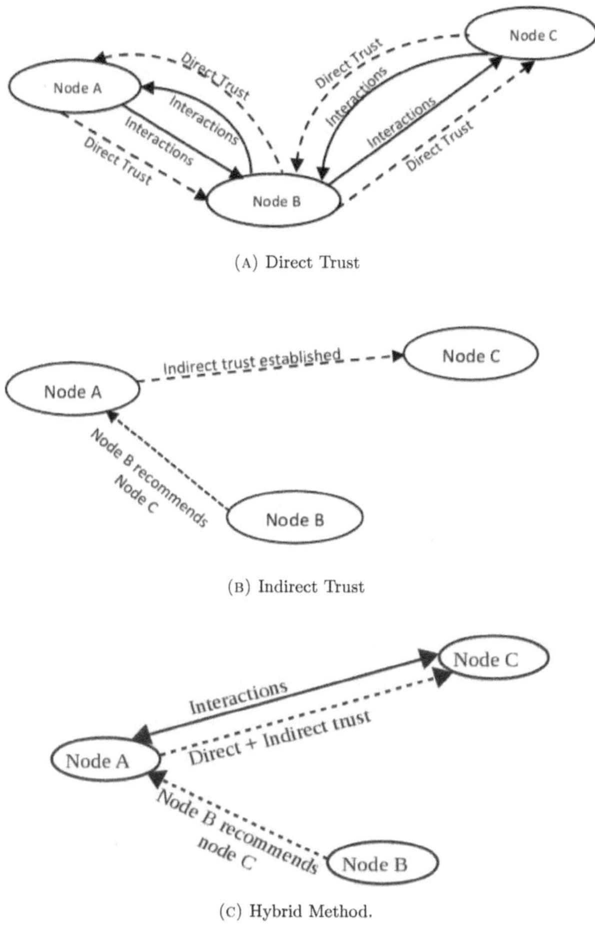

(A) Direct Trust

(B) Indirect Trust

(C) Hybrid Method.

FIGURE 2.1: Basic forms of Trust

Trust can be categorized into three major forms; direct, indirect and hybrid forms of trust. Direct trust is achieved by observing a neighbor directly, without involving a third party (figure 2.1a). On the other hand, the concept of trust transitivity is usually harnessed to establish indirect trust, which involves gathering recommendations from neighbors about a peer (figure 2.1b). The indirect trust of a trustee is dependent on the observation of other entities about its behavior during their past interactions. These observations are usually communicated to the trustor in form of recommendations.

There is also a hybrid of these two forms of trust. It involves the combination of direct and indirect trust to achieve even a stronger paradigm (figure 2.1c). This becomes particularly important when the trustor does not have enough information based on direct experience, to make decision concerning the trustee.

Security has been broadly classified into two categories; hard security and soft security [27]. Hard security is associated with the traditional security approaches such as traditional access control and authentication. It provides partial security; meaning that corporate resources are mainly protected from unauthorized users, but it does not always protect legitimate users from malicious service providers. This means that a central entity (usually the service provider) is able to assess peers that are requesting services, but the service requester nodes are not always empowered to assess such service provider in a distributed manner. Soft security tackles this weakness, and trust is often promoted as the basis for soft security [28].

2.1.1 Reputation

Reputation is usually the basis for determining trust, which implies that if an entity has maintained a good reputation during past interactions, it can gain a level of trust that would warrant subsequent interaction within a domain. Reputation can be seen as the view of other agents within a community regarding a given entity, which is generally known and assessed by the members of that community[29].

For nodes to communicate on trust platforms, it is necessary for them to be able to measure the level of trust they can place on each other. This influences the disposition of the nodes, to engage in transactions, or otherwise.

It can be challenging to measure digital trust with absolute precision, especially in distributed environments. The fact that many peers possess limited resources and capacities, adds to this challenge. Moreover, trust is a social concept, and some human instincts and reasoning which aid people in making trust decisions, are not easy to capture in algorithmic form. But the literature contains several approaches which have

been proposed for the purpose of aggregating and building trust in digital environments
[29]. Most of the proposals adopt one (or more) of the following methods to calculate
reputations, upon which trust is based.

1. *Summation*

   The simplest form of trust computation is usually to sum the positive and negative scores separately, then subtract the negative from the positive, in order to
   determine how reliable an agent has been. This approach has been adopted to
   calculate direct reputation in [11], and it is also used by eBay reputation system
   [30].

2. *Average*

   Another method which is close to simple summation involves taking the average of
   all scores of the peer being assessed, such as the case of Amazon [31]. Some other
   models such as TE-AODV [32] also use this method; assigning default scores to
   newcomers. Sometimes, this method is slightly extended, by taking the weighted
   average, instead of the normal average. The extended version allows the reputation
   of the recommending node (or similar factors) to be taken into account, as done
   in [8].

3. *Bayesian Method*

   Interaction outputs are usually rated as good or bad, that is, in a binary form.
   The number of positive and negative scores are used to compute reputation, using
   the beta probability density function (PDF). The PDF tuple α and β represent the
   number of good and bad interactions respectively, and the probability expectation
   value of beta distribution is represented as follows [33];

$$E(p) = \alpha/(\alpha + \beta) \tag{2.1}$$

   Compared to other methods, this method tends to have detailed theoretical back-
   ground which can amount to higher confidence in its outcome. During bootstrapping, α and β are each assigned the value of 1, which amounts to a default score
   of 0.5. Despite being popular, this type of (default) score initialization has been
   criticized for having the likelihood of being either unfair to the new node or the

ones that are already in the network. It also has a tendency of not adequately addressing white-washing [34, 35]. A white-washer is a peer that leaves the network, usually after behaving badly, and then rejoins with a different identity.

4. *Fuzzy Techniques*

This is one of the methods adopted for computing and aggregating reputation [8]. It involves reasoning about trust in-terms of fuzzy values. It appears to give more room for incorporating human-like reasoning such as agreement compliance, transaction time/age, etc, in reputation computation and aggregation. Given many recommendations for example, fuzzy technique can be applied to probe for the relevance of such recommendations by reasoning about compliance (or otherwise) to transaction agreement. That is, applying compliance as an objective measure to verify the subjective user ratings [36].

Sabater et al. [37] also falls under this category; they talked about the individual, social, and ontological dimensions of reputation. Individual and social dimensions correspond to direct and indirect trust respectively. But the ontological dimension dived deeper into what it actually means to have a given reputation. If company_A has a good reputation as a transportation company, then using fuzzy concepts, we may want to account for how it handles luggage, the kind of meal it serves, etc. Different techniques apply various means to capture trust, but fuzzy techniques appear popular in this kind of reasoning.

5. *Flow Techniques*

Here, reputation relates to the level of importance which a peer attracts within a community. As an example, in PageRank [38], the number of links pointing to an entity (such as website), compared to the number of links that leaves the entity, is used to determine the importance or reputation of that entity. If we take I(P) to be the set of other entities that are pointing to page P, otherwise called the in-links, and $|P|$ to be the number of other pages that P is pointing out to, otherwise called the outlink, then PageRank of P denoted by r(P), is computed as follows;

$$r(P) = \sum_{Q \in I(P)} \frac{r(Q)}{|Q|}, \tag{2.2}$$

where $|Q|$ is the out-links from Q. r(P) is mainly influenced by the pages that are pointing to it, which can be regarded as recommendations. However, an increase in the number of references made by Q, reduces the influence of Q on P.

6. *Belief Models*

This approach is somewhat related to probability theory, but the sum of 'probabilities' for all possible outcomes do not necessarily have to be equal to 1. Trust is expressed as a belief that a system will resist malicious attacks, or that a person will cooperate and not defect. A node is considered cooperative if it acts well, supporting and getting support from other nodes as expected. It defects when it begins to act selfish or malicious.

Unlike some other models in which belief in an agent's cooperation is considered true or false (i.e. discrete), belief models consider a case where there is no clear information on either belief or disbelief, and thus an uncertainty factor is introduced. Instead of using belief or disbelief in order to determine trust, uncertainty also counts. Opinions are usually expressed in the form [39]; $\omega_Y^X = (b, d, u, a)$, where ω_Y^X is X's opinion about statement Y, while b, d, and u stand for belief, disbelief, and uncertainty receptively. $a \in [0, 1]$ is referred to as relative atomicity, which is used to determine how uncertainty affects the expected opinion.

7. *Discrete Trust*

Trust is a social concept and thus humans as social entities are often better at determining the trust of other entities, based on experience and other intangible factors. Computationally, scholars try to capture as much of the human related attributes as they can, to enable them to make algorithmic trust possible and close to the human perception of trust. For example, some models such as [29] have emulated the human style of trust perception, to discreetly rank trust as very trustworthy, trustworthy, untrustworthy, very untrustworthy. Lookup tables are then used to determine the actual trust of an entity.

As outlined, trust logic comes in different forms. Our goal is not to apply all of them in our model, and we also do not think that doing so is necessary. We will however be taking advantage of some of the methods which have shown high prospects for success in the literature. This will be seen when we introduce the proposed method, but before we get there, it is important to discuss distributed networks and edge computing paradigms, as well as some known attacks in distributed networks. These are discussed subsequently.

2.2 Distributed Networks

TRS has been popularly applied to address security issues in distributed networks. In this section, we shall discuss some of the distributed networks, highlighting the ones that are of particular interest to this project, such as the mobile-edge clouds. Common attacks which the networks are vulnerable to, shall also be outlined.

Let us begin with Peer-to-peer (P2P) which is one of the most popular distributed protocols. P2P is a network architecture in which every node behaves in a similar way and renders same kind of service [9]. For example, nodes can function as clients and servers at the same time, making users more actively involved in the network, even offering their resources. P2P networks are popularly used for file sharing, but its application also spreads across various other domains, including the relatively new domain of edge computing. To illustrate how the network functions, we will now discuss popular P2P based protocols and other distributed network settings, paying particular attention to edge computing.

2.2.1 BitTorrent

BitTorrent is the most popular among P2P protocols, accounting for about 53% of the entire P2P traffic, and more than 30% of overall Internet traffic [40]. It is a good case study because it is very well known, widely deployed and it harbors major properties and behaviours of P2P systems. BitTorrent is mainly used for file/content sharing.

A share process in BitTorrent is initiated by first creating a meta-data describing the file that is to be shared, including SHA1 hash information about the pieces, among others. The information in the torrent file guides peers to the tracker and subsequently to other leechers and seeders in the swarm [41]. Leechers are peers that do not have all the file pieces, while seeders are peers with all the pieces. A tit-for-tat method is used to ensure that leechers who receive files also give to others. Seeders are assets to the network because they selflessly share files, without the need to download. Because of this, tit-for-tat does not directly apply to them and thus they can be exploited in some ways, as discussed subsequently.

In DHT (Distributed Hash Table) based BitTorrent, the tracker does not aid in the discovery of files or peerset. Nodes do this all by themselves. With distributed tracker systems such as Mainline DHT (MLDHT), peers use content IDs (also called infohash) to find the location of desired contents. Once a node knows the infohash of the file it wishes to fetch, it applies some controls to arrive at its location. Some of the controls include; 'PING' for ascertaining a node's availability, 'FIND_NODE' used to get the k-closest neighbors, 'GET_PEERS' for getting the initial peerset and 'ANNOUNCE_PEER' used by nodes to announce that they are part of the swarm [42]. Trust is usually required to empower nodes with some means of deciding who to transact with, or otherwise, without relying on central entities.

2.2.2 Edge Computing

This is a newer distributed computing paradigm. Computing trend went from main frame, which was mainly centralized, to personal computers which is a more distributed architecture. But centralization returned with cloud computing, before the recent shift back to decentralization due to the low latency requirements of IoT and related services. Edge computing paradigms such as fog computing, mobile edge computing, and mobile edge-clouds are all focused at ensuring low communication latency.

The centralization which cloud computing offers, has notable advantages. It provides the option of renting infrastructures, instead of a more expensive alternative of purchasing them, thereby making it less expensive to kick-start a businesses. Data collocation, abundant resources for heavy computations, on-demand, and elasticity are all parts of the advantages of cloud computing. It is a straightforward way to boost capacities and capabilities without the need to invest on new infrastructure, staff or software [43].

On the other hand, it is estimated that there will be about 50 billion connected devices by 2020 [44], and up to 1 trillion devices by 2025 [45]. Many of the devices will be generating several gigabytes of data within short intervals, which would need to be stored and processed. This would lead to sharp upward demand for bandwidth and thus become strenuous for the cloud computing infrastructure; especially because many IoT services require real-time update, and the cloud is remote in nature.

As an example, autonomous cars would be generating gigabytes of data per couple of miles or kilometers, which would require real time analysis or computation to enable them to navigate appropriately in real time. Connecting back and forth to the remote cloud would generate heavy traffic, and real time computation would be very difficult. Edge computing paradigms such as fog and mobile edge-clouds are distributed platforms, geared towards addressing latency and related issues.

Edge computing is a distributed architecture of information technology (IT) in which data processing is done at the network periphery; close to its originating source, as much as possible [46], as illustrated in Figure 2.2. The concept emerged around 2002, with main focus on application deployment over Content Delivery Networks (CDNs). Some companies aimed to take advantage of the resources and proximity of CDN edge servers to boost scalability [3]. Since then, edge computing concept has continued to evolve into different varieties and use-cases.

The advent of IoT has accelerated its growth, because resources which the edge devices already possess are capable of supporting the remote cloud if properly exploited. It can lead to latency reduction and faster service delivery, which is crucial for IoT applications. Our method is designed to be easily adaptable to edge computing platforms. More emphasis shall be on mobile edge-clouds because it is more distributed and can therefore be relatively more challenging to coordinate and secure, compared to some others. Different edge computing paradigms, which have been reported in the literature are outlined and discussed next.

2.2.2.1 Fog computing

Fog computing provides near-by data centers where some operations can be performed without the need to channel such process to the central cloud every single time. It provides networking, storage, and compute services between end devices (e.g. mobile devices) and traditional data centers. Fog nodes are heterogeneous devices that are distributed geographically - e.g. at roadside to monitor traffic related activities, and help autonomous cars to make real time decisions. Fog nodes can communicate with

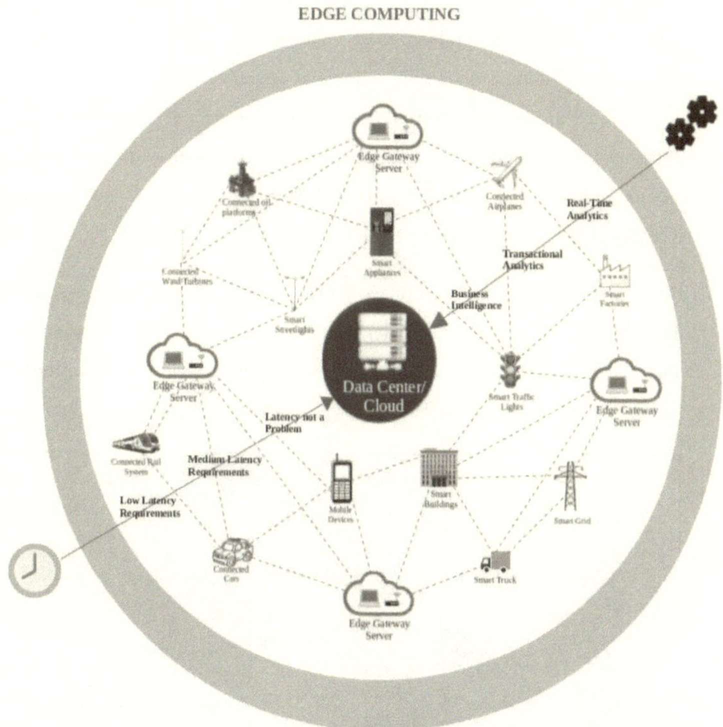

FIGURE 2.2: Edge Computing concept [1].

each other and with the cloud to share information. Under Fog, multiple infrastructure providers can coexist and cooperatively work with each other. Fog nodes and services launched on the cloud platform may belong to different actors including private users and mobile network operators [47]. Cisco defines Fog computing as "a paradigm that extends cloud computing and services to the edge of the network" [3].

With edge computing paradigms such as Fog, users can actually become part of a virtualization platform, able to lease out some storage or computing capacity for application to run on them. Fog requires the heterogeneous devices and services which run on its platform, to be managed homogeneously; in an automated fashion, using adequate software. The Network Function Virtualization (NFV) is a technology that makes the needed homogeneous management of heterogeneous devices and services achievable [44].

OpenFog Consortium is the body responsible for the standardization of fog computing. There are six groups established by Openfog for evaluation, classification and recommendation of standards, technologies and practices that are necessary to enable the fog architecture address its challenges adequately. In 2017, the OpenFog Consortium released the OpenFog Reference Architecture; a general framework designed with the intense data requirements of 5G, IoT and AI (artificial intelligence) applications in mind. It represents the first step in creating fog computing standards.

The framework presented in Figure 2.3 captures five key perspectives in fog computing, including; performance and scale, security, manageability, data analytic and control, and IT business and cross fog application perspectives [48]. Also captured are the three views that have been identified for fog, including software, system and node views.

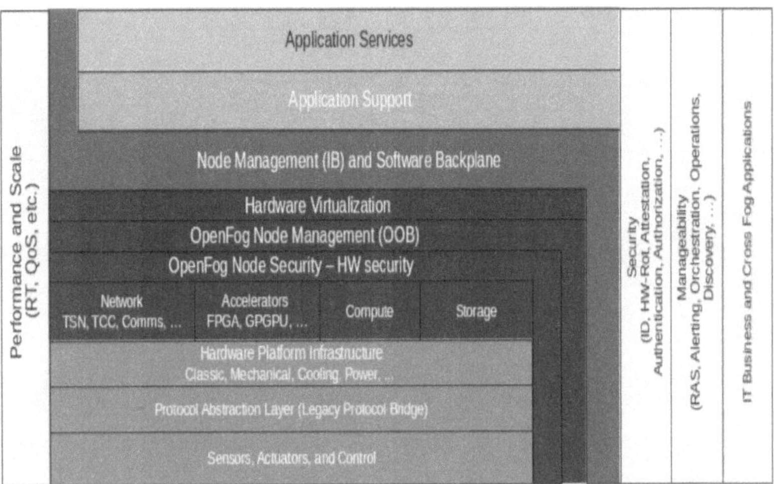

FIGURE 2.3: OpenFog Reference Architecture for Fog Computing [2].

2.2.2.2 Mobile Edge Computing (MEC)

Mobile edge computing is a similar concept to fog computing: it provides environment for IT services and cloud computing capabilities within Radio Access Networks (RAN), in close proximity to mobile subscribers. The aim is to reduce latency and improve efficiency in network operation and service delivery, thereby boosting user experience [49]. The IT service environment when brought to the network edge, will enable services and applications from mobile operators, content and service providers to be easily integrated into the multi-vendor MEC platform.

At the MEC world congress in 2016, Mobile Edge Computing was renamed as Multi-access Edge Computing, in order to accommodate non-cellular operators who also show huge interest in the concept [48]. MEC has been recognized alongside NFV and SDN (Software-Defined Networking) as key emerging technologies for 5G (5th Generation) networks. This is because it can help in transforming the mobile broadband network into a programmable world, while also contributing towards satisfying throughput, latency, automation and scalability, which are core requirements of the 5G.

With SDN, the logical overlay network can be decoupled from the underlying physical network [50]. This means that the logical overlay network can be programmed (changed, stored, etc.) without the need to reconfigure the associated physical hardware architecture. It can be leveraged to create and deploy innovative solutions that would address network-related issues, including congestion control, routing, or real-time communication.

MEC's approach is complementary to that of NFV, and both can be hosted on similar infrastructures. Technology integration, business transformation, and industry collaboration are the market drivers behind MEC. Augmented reality, intelligent video acceleration, connected cars, internet of things gateway are some service scenarios that stand to gain from Mobile Edge Computing [51]. But the requirements of 5G in the telecommunication firms remain the core business driver of MEC.

2.2.2.3   Cloudlet

A Cloudlet has been described as a "trusted" computer or a cluster of computers that are rich in resources, well connected to the Internet and is available for use by close-range mobile devices [48]. They are small data centers distributed geographically, closer to the mobile devices than the cloud. Cloudlet primarily aims at supporting resource intensive mobile applications, by providing mobile devices with powerful computing resources at low latency. It uses hand-off technology found in Virtual Machines (VM), to migrate offloaded services from one cloudlet to another as devices move from point to point.

OpenStack++, an extension of a more popular OpenStack has been implemented to support Cloudlets, in addition to other technologies such as cloudlet discovery, and just-in-time provisioning [48]. Cloudlet is less efficient compared to other advancements such as Mobile Edge Computing (MEC) due to its reliance on Wifi access points, and resource limitation of the Cloudlet servers [52, 53].

Cloudlet has also been identified as an approach to Mobile Cloud Computing (MCC), where mobile devices offload workload(s) to a local cloudlet, which is basically a set of multi-core computers connected to cloud servers. MCC is a general concept that captures offloading of tasks by mobile devices to the cloud computing infrastructures. This enables a mobile device to use resource providers, other than itself, to host application execution [54] - a concept which edge computing technologies share.

2.2.2.4   Edge-Centric Computing

This shares close similarity with the earlier mentioned methods, especially the Fog. Its bases are drawn from (i) the fact that individuals who upload documents to the cloud may be worried about loosing privacy over such documents to the central services, (ii) the zeal to exploit resources of emerging powerful mobile devices, and (iii) to close the gap that exist between man and machine, by focusing on human-driven applications that are controlled from the network edges. This "human centric" idea distinguishes it from other Edge computing methods.

Edge-Centric Computing aims to push data, applications, and services to the periphery of the network. It is envisaged that users, under this concept, are able to decide which part of their information a third party can access. The system is also expected to adapt to the behavior of any user, as well as handle interactions with humans via the connected mobile devices. Users can also be part of crowd-sourcing platforms by providing personal data for external use, such as allowing a third party company to access their energy usage data. The idea here is basically to make users more inclusive in the process [49] and minimize the man-machine gap.

2.2.2.5 Osmotic Computing

Similar to some other edge computing offshoots, this concept is motivated by the increasing need to support interactions between the IoT edge devices and the cloud. Osmotic computing is focused on the management of services across cloud and edge data centers in a dynamic manner, with the goal of improving QoS in IoT. More specifically, it is aimed at decomposing applications into micro-services, and then tailoring them dynamically in smart environments, utilizing both the resources available at the edge and the cloud. The idea is to have micro services in containers, and then move them opportunistically between the edge and the cloud, taking into account the condition of both infrastructures; in-terms of requirements like availability, reliability, and load balancing.

Osmotic computing tries to understand which service needs to be executed at the edge and that which needs to be executed at data centers. It hopes to dynamically handle resource contention among co-deployed micro-services across edge and the cloud. It is expected to detect and resolve resource contention through micro-service performance characterization, coordinated deployment and workload prioritization. Besides the well known method of offloading software applications from the edge devices to the cloud, osmotic computing holds the view of also enabling reverse upload for applications, from the cloud to the edge devices, to maintain a balance. According to [55], this can assist in checking latency and ensuring better resource management.

2.2.2.6 Mobile Edge-Clouds

Apart from the growing number of connecting devices, they (e.g. mobile devices) are also growing in capacity. Very often, users of those devices are found in close geographical proximity, presenting opportunities to tap into their collective resources. This is inline with the fact that availability, power efficiency, real-time demands, outage management, and even security can be better addressed by adopting the use of edge devices [56].

Mobile edge-clouds tap from that opportunity to pull various edge resources of end users together, to form a platform which is much higher in resources (compared to individual nodes) and on which computation and storage operations can take place. The idea is based on the fact that mobile devices are ubiquitous, and many possess considerable computation abilities which when put together can amount to a dependable platform for more powerful processing and storage abilities, than would be obtained in isolation. Individually, the devices are under utilized, less than 25% of their resources are engaged per hour [57]. Mobile edge-clouds can be of particular importance in cases of disaster or in huge crowds where bandwidth and latency could be issues [58].

Mobile edge-clouds can be totally comprised of near-by mobile devices with little or no infrastructural support [59]. It can also co-exist with traditional cloud computing, if need be [60]. It differs from similar concepts such as Cloudlet, Mobile Edge Computing (MEC) and Fog computing, which introduce mini servers to handle some storage and computational tasks instead of channelling all of them to/from the cloud. It is more distributed and thus presents more potential security challenges.

By providing storage and computation capabilities to the edge nodes, mobile edge-clouds can improve location and context aware decisions, reduce latency, conserve bandwidth, minimize cross-domain traffic, and also help to address some security and privacy concerns of traditional cloud computing; thereby improving Quality of Service (QoS). It can be equipped to serve low latency internet applications such as Robotics, virtual realities, and real time interactive industrial control systems. Since mobile edge-clouds does not replace cloud computing but co-exists with it, the cloud offers an infrastructure which edge-clouds agents can fall back to, if need be.

Mobile edge-clouds can be adapted for IoT applications or just conventional applications such as disaster recovery or improving user experience in a soccer stadium or content delivery, etc. It has also been identified as essential in attaining the emerging tactile internet which is aimed at interconnecting traditional (wired) network, mobile network and IoT, to form a unique kind of network [49]. IoT application may involve event detection, sensing, actuator controlled machine-to-machine interactions, or human-to-machine interaction. These usually generate huge data and traffic at the network edge, and necessitates aggregation and processing of such data at the same edge, so that only the aggregates are sent instead of the entire data which is heavier. This can reduce latency for real time machine-to-machine monitoring applications, and make provision for actuators and sensors who are resource and power constrained, to offload storage and computation to more powerful devices/platform.

Streaming applications and services over mobile edge-clouds' related platforms is beginning to gain patronage. Applications such as BitTorrent Live allows video streaming in a peer-to-peer form, without internet connection. Distributed storage is also beginning to take advantage of the platform: for example, Resilio Sync enables sharing of file over a private cloud through Wifi-Direct. Resilio Sync is deployed on top of BitTorrent protocol [61]. It has been shown that mobile edge-clouds can out perform the traditional cloud computing architecture, both in latency and power consumption efficiency [62].

Security of Mobile Edge-clouds: As a relatively new technology, edge computing and mobile edge-clouds in particular still face a number of challenges including, but not limited to privacy and security issues. For example, owners of mobile devices which are in close physical proximity, may be meeting themselves for the first time and have never communicated before. This makes everyone a stranger to its neighbors, with no pre-existing trust or endorsement from trusted agent. There is therefore a fundamental issue of trust.

Furthermore, participating nodes may be required to run codes from other devices in order to provide computational resources. This poses more threat than mere file exchange or running third-party applications, because third party applications are usually from known App stores which are subject to vetting. Nodes therefore need to be reassured before they can run such code, and that requires reasonable level of trust.

There is also an issue of privacy, considering the fact that mobile edge-clouds' nodes (devices) also provide data which are processed in the network, as well as storage and computation resources. Users contribute data/resources which they possess locally in their devices, such as videos, photos, contacts, location, etc. The privacy of such data is at stake and users worry about sharing privacy sensitive information. Because of these issues and related others, it is very challenging to adequately secure communication among entities in a mobile edge-clouds' platform [63].

2.3   Common attacks

Decentralized networks suffer from diverse forms of attack. Apart from free-riding, which is an act of selfishness, in which peers download from others without uploading to them in return, some other popular attacks in P2P (and similar networks) include the following:

1. *Lying Piece Attack*: The goal of this attack is to destabilize the 'rarest first' policy of file sharing platforms such as Bittorrent, in which peers while downloading, give priority to blocks that are scarce in the network, so that they will not be lost completely. Attackers advertise false pieces, thereby misleading other peers on the pieces that are actually rare [64]. More generally, the intention of attackers here might also be to cause other forms of confusion, such as diverting the attention of victims from genuine contents to non existing ones, in order to frustrate their download efforts.

2. *Chatty Peer Attack*: Attackers establish many TCP connections with their victims. They announce possession of many file pieces, but when the victims request for some blocks of such pieces, they never upload any. Instead, the attackers re-send handshake messages, thereby sticking as neighbors to the victims, who spend considerable amount of time waiting in vain for the attacker's response [65]. This can be an extension of the previous attack.

3. *Fake-Block Attack*: Attackers also advertise possession of many or all file blocks, pieces or packets. When victims request for such blocks, they send fake blocks in response. After downloading all blocks of a piece (from attackers and genuine peers), the victim may hash the file piece to check authenticity. This fails because of the fake blocks, warranting that the entire blocks be downloaded afresh, meaning a huge waste of bandwidth and time [66].

4. *Bandwidth Attack*: This is usually an attack targeted at service provider nodes (otherwise called seeders) with the goal of occupying their upload bandwidth, so that there is little or none left for legitimate peers. In protocols such as BitTorrent, seeders do not download, so they keep uploading to the fastest downloading peer(s). Attackers therefore exploit this by simply connecting to seeders and downloading only from them at fastest rate possible, so that they are constantly unchoked, while the reputable peers are continually choked [15, 16, 67]. This attack can extend to distributed networks in general, since a node can function as a service provider and/or service requester, depending on its status. *Node_A* is said to be unchoked by *Node_B* if *Node_B* is open to receive and service requests from *Node_A*, otherwise it is chocked.

5. *Sybil Attack*: Fake identities, otherwise called Sybils can be created very cheaply. To beat reputation systems, attackers create links between their Sybils, and through that means unleash different kinds of attack. They can also use such links for raising their own reputation and thus gain unmerited advantage [68, 69].

6. *Index Poisoning Attacker*: In distributed file sharing platforms for example, clients often keep indexes of files which map each file identifier to their hosts. Index poisoning attackers exploit this setting by publishing fake file indexes, with the goal of denying victims access to genuine neighbors. The attacker basically starts a file sharing task, but with fake information such as port number, IP address, infohash, etc. Since there are usually no strong verification means, owing to the openness of the system, this attack is easily executable. The innocent peers are left to pay the price by using up their time and resources trying to access contents (or packets) that are not truly existing; leading to denial of service [70].

7. *Combination Attack*: This is a form of content pollution attack, which combines fake-block and index poisoning attacks, to cause stronger effect. Attackers in this case extend index poisoning by including their own IDs in the fake infohash to be advertised. The idea is that if the victims insist on establishing connections despite failures due to fake information, they would eventually connect to the attacker(s) itself, who worsen their situation by feeding them with fake blocks. So they suffer the effects of both fake-block attack and index poisoning attack. Combination attack has been illustrated to impose more harm than fake-block or index poisoning attacks individually [71].

8. *Peer Exchange (PEX) Attack*: This is very similar to DDoS (Distributed Denial of Service) and index poisoning, it is sometimes captured separately to portray the fact that they are launched on PEX; taking advantage of its features such as large list of peers (upto 3000 in some cases), and very frequent PEX messages. Even though this is not the ideal design of PEX, studies have shown that almost all PEX implementations do not follow the original rules and there is no effective way to enforce it [72], making it easy for malicious peers to fabricate huge PEX peer lists with false IP addresses. This can cause victims to waste resources and time trying in vain to connect. Similarly, the attacker can also send PEX messages containing the address and port number of a victim to as many others as it can.

This is aimed at weighing the victim down with too many connection requests, resulting to DDoS.

9. *Collusion Attack*: Collusion attackers collude to favor themselves at the expense of legitimate peers. Attackers can join forces under collusion attack to make any of the mentioned attacks more devastating [73]. In TRSs, collusion attackers give themselves favorable scores, and downgrade the scores of others. This can mislead genuine peers into falsely believing that the malicious nodes are the reputable ones, and vice versa. With this method, the attackers can take over the network and successfully eliminate the genuine nodes from network services.

10. *Bad-mouthing [74] or Slandering [18] Attack*: These attacks both refer to an act of manipulating feedback or recommendations given concerning a given node, with the intention of reducing its reputation. It is common in nearly all distributed and semi-distributed TRSs. Recall that indirect trust score is obtained by asking for recommendations from neighbours who may have interacted with an unfamiliar agent. This helps the local node to make a decision regarding whether interaction with the agent is ideal or not. Via bad-mouthing or slandering attacks an innocent node may be shut out of the network as a result of false recommendations, especially when such attacks are coordinated directly or indirectly.

2.4 Summary

In this chapter, we discussed the concepts of trust and reputation. The "controversy" in the definition of trust was highlighted, and different forms of trust were explained. The meaning of reputation and different ways of computing reputation were outlined. Distributed networks were equally discussed using various protocols. BitTorrent was introduced to highlight the properties of a traditional P2P platform, while edge computing represents recent and emerging offshoots of distributed networks; we highlighted how edge computing paradigms are crucial to the future of computing. Security challenges and common attacks were also explored; these attacks are potentially applicable to edge computing.

Chapter 3

State of the Art

The literature reports many TRS (Trust and Reputation System) proposals that seek to ensure trust and security in distributed networks. In this chapter, we have reviewed such reports, highlighting their strengths and weaknesses, so that we can build on them to derive a better solution. We covered popular distributed environments including P2P, MANETs, blockchain, bittorrent and edge computing.

3.1 Trust Bootstrapping, Propagation, Aggregation and Prediction

This section outlines the popular methods which are used to compute trust in Trust and Reputation Systems (TRSs). The methods which shall be discussed in subsequent sections apply one method or the other to bootstrap, propagate, and aggregate trust information, enabling nodes to predict the likelihood of compliance (or otherwise) of other peers. The idea here is to give an overview of how trust computation works generally in TRSs, so that subsequent discussions would make more sense. We shall in the following sections describe different TRS based methods that have been proposed for different distributed environments, including P2P, blockchain, and MANET.

- Bootstrapping: The first method often involves trust bootstrapping, which addresses how newcomers are going to be introduced into the network, in a safe and efficient manner. Generally, the literature approaches this in six different ways.

The first and most popular method involves assigning default or positive values to newcomers [8, 10, 75]. The second is the dynamic initialization method [76], in which the current security status of the network (or system) determines the scores that would be assigned to the new nodes. If maliciousness is currently high, then the value of initial trust score will be low, otherwise it would be high.

Thirdly, there is a recommendation and endorsement based method. Under this category, if a newcomer has similar interest and capabilities [34] or patterns [35], with an existing service (or node) which is already known as credible, then its initial score can be derived from such existing node or service. The fourth involves the use of game theory [77] for predicting initial trust, usually in web service platforms. Method number five involves the use of central/super entities [78], or prior registration [79], or pre-existing trust relationship [80, 81].

The sixth method features the use of challenge/puzzle [82, 83] to restrict the number of fake identities that a Sybil attacker can introduce into the network. This is more related to resource testing rather than trust. It is easy for existing nodes to verify puzzles, but an attacker can outsource the puzzle computation and then introduce many Sybils into the network; this is obviously not good for the existing nodes who unknowingly clear such Sybil entities. Our method is different because emphasis is not only on resources but also on reputation, during and after the bootstrap stage. The new method is also distributed, with no need for prior registration, pre-existing trust relationship or super node.

- Propagation: Guha et al. and Zhang et al. [84, 85] specifically highlighted the importance of trust propagation in TRS. To give an example of how this process works, in [84] trust is propagated based on the length of arguments: If i trusts j, and j trusts k, then in one propagation step (otherwise known as atomic propagation) the possibility of i trusting k could be inferred. This is based on the transitive attribute of trust. According to Zhang et al. [85], if graph C represents the network that contains all possible trust relationships which can be formed through trust propagation, such that the observed network N is a sub-graph of C (That is; if a vertex set $U(N)$ of network N is the same with vertex set $U(C)$ of network C, and an edge set $E(C)$ of N is contained in $E(C)$ of C) then C is considered a candidate network. Given any vertices (u,v), if such vertices do not form an edge in network C, then it is impossible for u to trust v through trust propagation.

Most TRSs use propagation techniques that are similar to that of [84]. In general, a web of trust can be formed by exploiting the transitivity attribute of trust.

- Aggregate: After propagation, there is usually the need to aggregate trust information. The literature has reported a number of trust aggregation approaches, such as GossipTrust and CMANET explained in [27]. GossipTrust focuses on fact aggregation while CMANET draws its bases from distributed Bellman-Ford algorithm which is considered sophisticated, and thus best used for light weight aggregations in order to avoid incurring heavy overhead. The authors of [86] also focused on the lying strategies of recommendation givers during the aggregation process. They explained that provision needs to be explicitly made for these lying strategies by Beta-family TRS models.

  In general, a good TRS should be able to efficiently sieve out bogus information resulting from propagation (e.g. recommendation). This is done in a number of ways; some systems simply sum or take an average of recommendations, others probe into how genuine they are via different means. In the previous chapter, we discussed various methods through which reputations are aggregated to arrive at trust.

- Prediction: The aim of propagating and aggregating trust information is to actually build trust in a reliable way. In [87] an opportunistic network was used to illustrate this, while in some other models, nodes use the ratio of packets that were correctly forwarded by neighbours to determine its trust history [88]. Fuzzy logic (or similar approach) can also be applied, with the evaluated node's trust history and its ability to deliver services credibly, as inputs.

  Hopefully the term 'prediction' did not sound confusing, it was used to capture the idea of decision making based upon the trust information already gathered. For example, an agent may determine (or 'predict') with some level of certainty that another party would act in a given way (favourable or otherwise).

  Often times, a node's direct experience tend to supersede or totally eclipse trust information that is gathered through other means, because the node trusts itself better than others in the network. However, getting a global opinion is crucial, so that nodes do not keep acting based on local view. A good approach is usually to combine the two (local and global views) and then determine how much weight to attach to each, based on defined heuristics.

3.2 TRS in Peer-to-Peer (P2P)

This section discusses popular related works in the P2P domain. It is one of the popular distributed networks where TRS has been heavily featured. Studying TRS in P2P is essential for understanding how it would be adapted to work better in emerging offshoots such as mobile edge-clouds.

Naghizadeh et al. [11] proposed a model which targets free-riding and similar attacks in BitTorrent, a popular P2P protocol. In their system, the tracker serves as a super node, helping other nodes to make decisions that would help them to avoid free-riders. The authors of [66] came up with a more decentralized method in which 10 percent of the nodes act as super-nodes, and are charged with the responsibility of decision making. However, there is a possibility of some malicious nodes making it to the super node stage, and then taking advantage of the network. Moreover, this method also relies on central agents.

The work of Shah et al. [89] shares significant similarity with the method proposed by Sarjaz and Abbaspou [66]. The former randomly selects peers whose scores would be used to compute the global scores, not the top 10 percent, as mentioned earlier. The idea in both cases is that by having the view of other nodes, collusion attack would be averted. But that is true only if the views of sincere nodes are considered in computing the global score, otherwise the computed score would be deceptive. The random choice in this method makes it difficult to survive certain percentage of maliciousness; the system stops being efficient when the number of malicious nodes grows up to 30 percent.

Wong et al. [12] mainly focused on content pollution. For any pollution suspected, the network is divided into subunits in order to identify and carve out pollutants. This technique can cause huge overhead and possible isolation of network segments. In the same vein, Santos et al. [90] proposed a reputation voting system based on subjective logic, where peers are required to vote for files as either polluted or valid. However, vote collection can take time, since the nodes might need to download big chunk of the file before casting their votes.

In [90], when a node finishes downloading a content/file, it gives a positive or negative vote for that content, to reflect how valid (or otherwise) the file is. When the reputation for a given content is beyond a threshold, then it is considered non-polluted and downloads are encouraged. A tracker is used here to regulate concurrent downloads, but their approach does not work for DHT and PEX (Peer Exchange) based systems since they depend on a central agent.

An automatic voting system with similar concept and assumption was proposed in [91] to incentivize nodes and make them willing to vote, so that reliable information may be gathered concerning each content/file. The system assumes that files which are seeded frequently have high reputation and are not polluted, while the ones that are deleted after download are most likely contaminated. Machine learning algorithms were used to learn about this, but the claim is only implicit, not proven to work. The main focus appears to be on the whole file, not chunks or pieces which are exchanged to build up the file. However, attackers may be able to embed malicious or bogus block(s) at piece level, causing a file which is valid to be considered malicious.

Pecori's work [75] focused on Sybil attacks within Kademlia-based BitTorrent protocols. Nodes assess their potential service providers based on trust scores. In particular, trust scores are taken into account when selecting/ordering the k-bucket. Newcomers are kick started with some positive risk scores to enable them join the network. Kohnen [92] also focused on Kademlia with similar approach, but each peer has a trust management node which must be contacted whenever the trust score of such peer need to be accessed.

These methods reflect the trend in most reputation and trust models, which involves placing emphasis mainly on client nodes, in order to shield them from malicious server nodes, but with minimal emphasis on protecting the server nodes (seeders) from greedy leechers. This creates room for bandwidth attack, which has received little or no attention in current trust and reputation models. Bandwidth attack is mainly targeted at seeders, not leachers. A few methods which are not reputation or trust based have attempted to address the bandwidth attack, but suffer crucial limitations related to poor or nonexistent means of verifying claims/votes [67], and outrageous overhead due to frequent encryption and decryption operations [93].

Another trend that is easily noticeable is the fact that most of TRS bootstrap trust by assigning initial trust (or risk) score which does not reflect the newcomer's behavior, and which may be unfair to either the existing nodes or the newcomer. The reports in [8] and [10] also feature in this trend, and initialize newcomers with scores that allow them to join the network without initial assessment, thereby making whitewashing very easy. A white-washer would leave the network (e.g. when its trust score drops) and then rejoins with a different identity.

Some exceptions to the default trust score trend, such as [94] and [95] require bootstrapping servers for new nodes to join, which can be a bottleneck in distributed settings. Other methods [80] require some form of 'pre-established' trust relationship for newcomers, which may not always be available. An alternative solution which is based on the Opennet model [80] allows publicly known 'seednodes' to assist in introducing new nodes. However, this might involve revealing vital information to malicious nodes too, which they can use to attack the network. Additionally, if for any reason a 'seednode' becomes malicious, its effect would be high because of its high privilege.

Danezis et al. [81] proposed a system that would be resistant to Sybil attacks. It is also based on pre-established trust relationship, which can be unavailable in some cases. Such relationships are expected to have been acquired offline, and are accumulated to form a bootstrap graph, which is a core part of their modified DHT routing mechanism.

We provide a summary of related work regarding TRS in P2P, in Tables 3.1 and 3.2. In Table 3.2, 'Y' stands for 'yes', '-' represents 'no', 'NA' means 'Not Applicable', while 'P' is for 'partial'. Our views about Sybil attack as reflected on the table agrees with an earlier work in [69], and more recently [75] which noted that no effective Sybil attack measure has been derived for distributed networks. We used the term 'partial' to mean that the reviewed method can minimize the attack, but not stop it completely. While 'yes' indicates those we think have addressed them more directly. Methods that focus only on bootstrapping were discussed in the previous section.

3.3 TRS in Edge Computing

A number of reports have also suggested the use of TRS particularly in edge computing. Some of them include [58] which proposes a mechanism that requires people (eg. administrators) to actually visualize the contents of a packet/file and sign them, before dissemination. However, this can be laborious, and as traffic grows, scalability can be a

TABLE 3.1: Summary of related work

Reference	Strength	Weakness
Qureshi et. al. [7]	Provides copyright protection.	Pre-trusted and central entities are required, and they may not always be available.
Aringhieri et. al. [8]	Provides effective aggregation system.	It can be resource intensive due to broadcasts.
Cornelli et. al. [9]	Provides partial anonymity, which gives a level of privacy.	Not accountable for peers that drop requests, which would discourage cooperation.
Kamvar et. al. [10]	Scores reflect global view and therefore more likely to be valid.	Pre-trusted peers have to be trusted always. If they become malicious, the entire system suffers.
Naghizadeh et. al. [11]	Mitigates free-riders efficiently.	Scores are sieved poorly, this would make them prone to easy manipulation.
Sarjaz et. al. [66]	The reputation of recommending nodes are assessed, this would make malicious nodes to have less impact in the score computation.	Rogue nodes might make it to the top/super level, and hijack the network.
Adamsky et. al. [67]	Nodes are able to make independent decisions.	Fake votes can easily be given.
Ragab-Hassen et. al. [96]	Vote falsification is difficult.	It can be resource intensive.
Santos et. al. [90]	Nodes are able to make assessments early enough, which leads to quicker decision making.	It is not DHT compatible.
Ormandi et. al. [91]	Scoring can be automatic and quick.	The system is only implicit, not tested.
Wong et. al. [12]	Tracks pollution or maliciousness at block level.	Tracker could be overworked/overwhelmed leading to potential denial of service.
Dhungel et. al. [13]	Fake pieces can be detected easily.	False positive/negative can be high.
Pecori R. [75]	Can function in distributed platforms.	The system only manages the effects of Sybil attack, not addressing it fully.
Clarke et. al. [80]	Trust bootstrapping was considered here.	When pre-relationship in unavailable, the alternative can be weak.
Danezis et. al. [81]	Routing can be done safely with this system.	Newcomers require pre-trusted peers.
FBit	Distributed, efficient bootstrapping, bandwidth attack mitigation.	Churn effect not analyzed.

TABLE 3.2: Summary of related work II. Here is a description of the columns: 'Boot Perf' captures whether trust was bootstrapped or not, while 'Distributed' refers to how distributed the system is. Accordingly, 'Content Pollution' and 'Selfish Acts' reflect how the system handles content pollution and selfish acts such as free-riders respectively. 'Sybil Attack' and 'Bandwidth Attack' also account for how much the system addresses the respective attacks. 'Y' stands for 'yes', '-' represents 'no', 'NA' means 'Not Applicable', while 'P' is for 'partial'.

Reference	Boot Perf	Distributed	Content Pollution	Selfish Acts	Sybil Attack	Bandwidth Attack
[7]	-	-	Y	-	P	-
[8]	-	Y	Y	Y	P	-
[9]	-	Y	Y	Y	P	-
[10]	-	Y	Y	Y	P	-
[11]	-	-	Y	Y	P	-
[66]	-	-	Y	Y	P	-
[67]	NA	Y	-	-	-	Y
[96]	-	Y	Y	Y	P	-
[90]	-	-	Y	P	P	-
[91]	-	-	Y	P	P	-
[12]	-	-	Y	Y	-	-
[13]	-	Y	Y	Y	P	-
[75]	-	Y	Y	Y	Y	-
[80]	Y	Y	Y	Y	Y	-
[81]	Y	Y	-	Y	Y	-
FBit	Y	Y	Y	Y	Y	Y

serious issue. Huang et al. [97] also presented an architecture in-which the cloud acts as a security enabler in MANET or mobile cloud. Services such as trust pre-establishment are considered to be beyond the MANET, and are thus provided by the cloud. Such dependency on central points brings about latency-related concerns.

Similarly, Dybedokken [98] proposed a trust management system for fog, where the trust model runs on the fog nodes and the fog clients only get the end result. Schooler et al. [99] reiterated the importance of blockchain application as well as brokerage system that would reconcile the compliance of objects in an IoT fog environment. Mobile edge-clouds' nodes are more independent compared to fog computing clients; these methods and similar others which are built around the hierarchical nature of fog may not be good fit, mainly because mobile edge-clouds is less hierarchical.

3.4   TRS in Blockchain Systems

In this section, a review of the application of TRS in blockchain systems is documented. This is necessary because we are interested in merging Blockchain with TRS, to derive a blockchain-based system that would be IoT friendly.

Although there are many reputation based methods which are aimed at providing trust and security in distributed networks, reports that focus on safeguarding the reputation scores upon which TRS is based, are relatively not so many. Scholars have quickly identified blockchain as a way of addressing the challenge. They have also illustrated the fact that TRS can equally help to improve trust, security and cooperation in blockchain systems.

In this section we shall highlight both reports: where blockchain is employed to secure TRS scores, and where TRS is employed to make blockchain even more resilient. This is relevant because we shall be adapting our model into blockchain, mainly to secure the trust scores. According to Lu et al. [100], the security of a reputation system is in itself a serious challenge that is still unresolved. Lu's work focused on the issue related to privacy, using a kind of central monitoring agent. They proposed a method that features an enforcement agent and a certificate authority, which approves and issues certificates respectively.

Khaqqi et al. [101] introduced blockchain technology into emission trading scheme, which is aimed at reducing emission and encouraging the adoption of technologies that encourage long-term abatement. They acknowledged that Blockchain can ensure immutability of recorded data but cannot guarantee that the original data entered into a system is credible, since such data may have been generated via other channels. They used smart tamper-resistant meters to ensure that inputs are obtained correctly. In their system, participants are able to access offers based on their reputations. More reputable ones are able to get more offers, while those with less reputation can only get limited offers. This works because the (reputation-based) trading rules are incorporated into the blockchain, accessible by all.

Yu et al. [102] also applied the concept of reputation to Blockchain. They focused on strengthening the Blockchain network to be able to withstand attacks even if the attackers make up to 51 percent of the network. The reputation of a miner is derived based on how much it contributes to the network. The reputation of each node with respect to the total reputation of the network determines the weight of its vote during consensus. Leaders who do not commit up-to 'x' miniblocks (transactions) per epoc (time) may be penalized for under performing, this is in attempt to ensure that it does not stall the throughput. The time required for reputation to be built, makes it difficult for resourceful nodes to instantly hijack the network. This work focuses on applying reputation system to strengthen the blockchain system. But as discussed later in this work, part of our focus will be on securing the reputation system itself, using blockchain technology.

Sharples et al. [103] suggested a blockchain of intellectual achievements and reputation, such that it can be used for employment, academic recognition and even have trade-able (monetary) values. Students and institutions alike can earn badges and kudos based on their contributions and performances. This can be recorded in the Blockchain to make it publicly available and verifiable. The University of Nicosia already offers certificates that can be verified via Bitcoin Blockchain[1], which may be considered a primary step to the ideas of Sharples et al. We share in their idea of adding more value to reputation: a situation where the reputation of agents (e.g. persons or nodes) would be globally known is envisaged. There may be a problem of determining a uniform (cross platform) reputation measure, but that may be resolved with further research.

In another related work, Yang et al. [104] proposed a blockchain based trust management system for vehicular networks, with focus on assessment, dissemination and recording of trustworthiness in the network. They assumed that only a small number of attackers may be present in the the network, and therefore their impact via bad-mouthing may be insignificant. Each vehicle is expected to go through the RSUs (Roadside Units) before they are able to access the trust information of neighbors. The RSUs are also exclusively responsible for trust computation and reaching consensus. On the contrary, we shall focus on a different kind of network and do not envisage only a small number of attackers. We will also be looking at a system that would allow each peer to directly access the trust information of any other node in the network. In addition, we intend to store less detail in the public ledger to make it less bulky.

---

[1]https://digitalcurrency.unic.ac.cy/free-introductory-mooc/self-verifiable-certificates-on-the-bitcoin-blockchain/ academic-certificates-on-the-blockchain/ (Accessed 12/12/2018).

In [105], an obligation chain was introduced, where obligations can be published and can be used to judge the trust of an entity. They are focused on trust between islands of trust, while assuming that each TRS island is locally secure. The system is made up of service provider (SP), service provider end-device (SPD), service provider back-end server (SPB), service consumer (SC), service consumer end-device (SCD), and service consumer back-end server (SCB). The SPB publishes terms while the SCB is responsible for keeping track of changes that may occur in the terms. The medium for publishing the terms is not exactly specified, but a website was suggested. SPB further accesses SCs and decides whether the SP should trust them or otherwise. Based on the terms, SCB creates and signs obligations. After verifying the obligations, the SPB sends a Bitcoin account where SC would pay for services received. Unlike their method, our system is focused on addressing security challenges within a distributed trust island. It is focused on less organized systems such as mobile edge-clouds, where infrastructures can be limited or absent.

Schaub et al. [106] suggested a system that uses blockchain to attain privacy in online TRS systems. Users can publish reviews anonymously so that other users can analyze such reviews before transacting with a service provider. They aim to eliminate the need for encryption key. There were no means of reaching agreement on the trustworthiness of peers: individuals publish reviews which may be divergent. Similarly, only service providers can be rated, not the consumers or clients. Wealthy service providers are also able to easily undertake ballot-stuffing. Moreover, no method of public key distribution, from service providers to clients, was mentioned.

The report of [107] contains a feedback system that gives vouchers to customers as incentive for positive feedback. The feedback (if signed) adds reputation to the service provider up to the voting fee which the provider proposed in the voucher. Wealthy service providers can have more reputation since they can afford higher voting fees, and they can also assign vouchers to fake identities to promote their reputation. Also, if services are free, the providers will still have to pay for the reputation even without receiving any money for the service.

Targeting BitTorrent specifically, Pant et. al. [108] suggested a system that rewards file upload based on Bitcoin. They aim to combat free-riding, arguing that with crypto-currency incentives, nodes would rather contribute than become a free-rider. Their system requires a certificate authority which confirms every Bitcoin address that is to participate in the system. Peers are also required to report to another central agent, each time they upload a file, so that they can get their pay. These factors make it unsuitable for more distributed platforms such as Kademlia. Whether a Bitcoin gained in this manner is equivalent or comparable to that which is gained through the traditional mining process is also not clear.

In [18], the authors aimed at addressing similar problem which has to do with how information regarding trust can be shared without bias or modification. Each time a file is received, the receiver sends the information to the miners who contact the two nodes involved in that transaction, asking them to send a signed proof: a nonce sent by the miner, and the file hash. Apart from sending transaction information to the miners, nodes also store more details locally. To make the chain lighter and increase transaction per second, transactions that are more than 30 days old are deleted by the miners. Nodes connect to miners to ask for information concerning any peer that they may wish to download from. This work was mainly theoretical, and appears only partially distributed because peers are not able to make independent decisions.

Like in [106] and similar others, [18] allows clients to judge service providers based on the quality and authenticity of the files they share. But service providers lack bases to credibly judge the clients in a way that can stop malicious clients from exploiting them. Interaction rates are mainly downplayed; according to the authors, one transaction between two nodes is same as a thousand transactions in-terms of reputation. Only 10 transactions per second is possible with their system (theoretically), and it is expected to handle up to 40 percent of attackers. Impact of Sybil attack on the system was not ascertained, and they stated that more work would be needed to make the system function in BitTorrent and similar networks. Our work partly aims to address this weakness by incorporating blockchain-based reputation system into mobile edge-clouds, BitTorrent and similar platforms.

3.5   TRS in other Distributed Platforms

Here, we are going to highlight popular TRS schemes that are used in similar other distributed platforms, such as MANET. This helped us to further establish the pattern which TRSs follow in making trust decisions, as earlier outlined.

In [109], a Reputation-Based Framework for Sensor Networks (RFSN) was reported. It has two major components; watchdog system which identifies outliers, and reputation system which has the responsibility of keeping track of the reputation of every node. A stationary reputation state is expected to be reached through a considerable high number of interactions before a trust decision can be possible: this can be considered its main downside.

The distributed network monitoring approach proposed by Lopez et al. [110] focuses on reconciling trust issues between DNS and client systems. The work aims at enhancing trust in the responses which DNS servers give, by combining information from various observation points to arrive at a more accurate trust result. It is focused on communication between a client computer from a remote location (such as a hotel that has public internet connection) and an authoritative DNS server of a company via a catching DNS server (of the hotel); ensuring that information reaching the client computer remains consistent with the one from the company's server.

A Trust Based Encryption (TBE) was introduced in [111] to ensure privacy during information sharing in distributed networks. According to the report, a sender needs a reputation value (R) during encryption while the receiver needs to have a separate key which must tally with a rating value (r), such that $r \leq R$. This system in practice would incur huge communication overhead, and could be cost intensive.

Consequently, Lin et al. [112] proposed a modified trust based encryption (TBE) scheme which features reduced communication overhead and memory management with similar privacy level. Both approaches assumed central key systems, which can be a cause for concern.

In [113], nodes directly monitor their one-hop neighbors based on two behaviors; packet modification and packet dropping. The assumption here is that the nodes overhear each other, enabling them to know if packets are delivered to designated nodes without mutilation, or otherwise. Trust scores are calculated afterwards based on Bayesian inference and Dempster Shafer theory. The idea behind this work is that only the shortest path nodes are observed, not every node. After finding the shortest path nodes, they are registered using fuzzy logic, and service request(s) are sent to them. It is not clear whether (or not) the system is able to differentiate when packets are dropped for any other reason besides maliciousness, such as resource issues or energy.

Similarly, Wang et al. [114] is focused on dynamic trust estimation for service provider nodes with peculiar consideration to their behavioral pattern as they respond to environmental changes. They opined that trustworthy service providers (SP) will be more likely to be selected by many service requesters (SR), since the nodes that enjoy their trustworthiness will usually propagate their observations to the rest of the nodes in the network. The novelty of their work is the introduction of logistic regression into trust computation as against the popular Bayesian and fuzzy logic. It may however be resource intensive, in-terms of processing time and storage.

In a nutshell, they are focused on predicting the future behaviour of a node based on recommendations received concerning that node and the environmental conditions (e.g. energy, capability) surrounding those recommendations. This is done as a way of getting a balanced view of the node's behaviour, from the recommendations, as much as possible. We addressed similar concerns using similarity check (see subsection 4.6.1), and plan to possibly eliminate the risk altogether by adopting some blockchain attributes.

Venkanna et al. [32] focused on dynamic calculation of trust and available energy value of each node, and applying results in cooperative routing path establishment. They grouped node behavior into two; malicious nodes and selfish nodes. Malicious nodes modify packets and disrupt routing patterns, thus yielding attacks like greyhole attack and blackhole attack among others. Selfish nodes do not really cause any attack, but they only communicate when transactions would favor them, else they choose to reserve their resources and not spend it on helping others. Similar to the other methods, authors assume an initial score for newcomers.

A black hole node basically forges routing information such as the number of hops and sequence number, falsely claiming to be the destination node. As a result, packets can be routed to it in error, and it would be able to eavesdrop and then drop the packets. [115]. Gray hole nodes selectively drop packets, instead of dropping all as black hole attackers do [116].

In [117], the use of certificates and trust management were combined for secure routing in MANET. Certificates are needed for nodes to gain access, and afterwards, trust management is deployed to monitor its behavior: This approach falls within the fifth method of trust bootstrapping, based on our earlier classification. Each node evaluates the information gathered by self and neighbor nodes, to aid its trust decisions. Trust management here comprises of information gathering, scoring, and response. Assessment and evaluation of direct and indirect observations make scoring possible. Management of certificates in a distributed way can be challenging.

3.6 Summary

Detailed literature review of existing reports has been presented. We looked into various P2P protocols and similar networks including MANETs. BitTorrent, mobile edge-clouds, and blockchain technologies are also among the distributed networks which have been reviewed, focusing on the application of TRS to achieve network security in a distributed or semi distributed manner. Strengths and weaknesses of TRSs in these areas were highlighted, establishing the bases and need for the proposed system. The proposed method builds on the strength of the literature, while closing its gaps; leading to a system that would serve both emerging edge computing paradigms such as mobile edge-clouds, and older distributed protocols such as BitTorrent.

Chapter 4

FBit (Fairer Bits)

The proposed system is termed FBit (Fairer Bits); it is aimed at improving fairness and robustness against maliciousness in distributed networks, with focus on bandwidth attack, fake block attack, free-riding, sybil attack and collusion attack. FBit ensures that peers are treated with priorities that match their levels of cooperation, thereby providing better motivation for cooperation, better resource management, network safety, fairness and efficiency. Although a modified BitTorrent protocol has been used for illustration, mainly due to its popularity and similarity to some use-cases of mobile edge-clouds, the new method can be applied to other distributed platforms as highlighted subsequently. This chapter explains the FBit system and experimental results obtained. It also contains detailed explanations of how various components of the system work.

4.1   Reputation Bootstrapping

At the point of entry, every node is expected to generate a key pair (K_p, K_b) with which they sign their transactions. New nodes start by discovering other nodes that are already in the network through the tracker (or DHT) as in normal BitTorrent, and then sending Bitfield messages requesting to be added as neighbors. Through the messages (or controls), they also send their self signed certificates. When a trustor receives such request, it associates the accompanying public key with the trustee, to distinguish it from other nodes. A trustor is a node who decides whether or not to trust another peer, the trustee. Node's ID can be derived from its public key (e.g. taking a hash). For the newcomer's request to be granted, it has to demonstrate some preliminary trustworthy acts.

As an illustration, assume that *nodeA*, *nodeC* and *nodeE* were already in the network, when *nodeB* requests to join through *nodeA*. After *nodeB's* request, when *nodeA* receives the next unchoke message from any of its neighbors (e.g. *nodeC*), it responds by sending a request for a block, according to BitTorrent procedure. However, in addition, it requests that the block should be routed through *nodeB* (which is the new node), instead of having it sent directly. When *nodeB* receives such block from *nodeC*, it forwards it to *nodeA*, appending its signature, based on the key it generated initially. Note that the block by itself is not intelligible. For it to make sense, other blocks that make-up a piece must be received too. The newcomer is however unable to determine the blocks which it receives, and it would most likely receive random blocks from different pieces, which would only make sense if it is able to join the network and request the missing ones.

Given that the transaction is honest, *nodeB* gains some reputation points, and the reputation of *nodeC* is updated too. This ensures that the new node does not gain reputation advantage over the existing ones. *NodeA* can repeat this step for some other blocks, giving *nodeB* more opportunities to serve and build reputation. In case of DHT, proximity would be considered in the routing process, such that nearby nodes would be more active in helping the newcomer to gain reputation.

While *nodeA* is waiting, it can proceed with other requests so that it would not be trapped if *nodeB* does not deliver. Other nodes in the network such as *nodeC* and *nodeE* (who are now aware of the newcomer) can also route some of their requests through *nodeB*, thereby giving it quick chances to build up reputation and join the network fully. The new node is not allowed to request any service until it is admitted. Each transaction, both from the new and old nodes are signed. Relying on the reputation of the existing node(s) which are introducing the newcomer, we assume that they will act fairly. To be precise, nodes with low trust scores will not be able to introduce a newcomer. Based on their trust scores, we can be hopeful that they would treat the new nodes fairly. Existing nodes can lose reputation for inappropriate introduction, and can also gain for appropriate ones.

When *nodeB* joins through multiple nodes (e.g. *nodeA*, *nodeC*, *nodeE*), *nodeA* determines if *nodeB* is due to be added as a neighbor, by collecting recommended Bootstrap factors (Bf) from the other nodes. *NodeA* further weighs each recommendation based on its trust on the nodes that sent them, as illustrated in equation (4.1). Bf_{CB} is the Bf reported by *nodeC* concerning *nodeB*, while GS_{AC} is the reputation of *nodeC* from the perspective of *nodeA*. The same pattern repeats for every neighbor that would submit Bf recommendation. Notice that *nodeA* still adds its own bootstrap factor, which it computed previously (Bf_{AB}), but with an optimal self reputation of 1. Bf_{A_B} is the current *Bf* of B, calculated by A. It will be used as Bf_{AB} in the next update of *Bf* for node B, if need be.

$$Bf_{A_B} = \left(\sum_C Bf_{CB} \cdot GS_{AC} \right) + Bf_{AB} \tag{4.1}$$

No further normalization is relevant at this stage because the newcomer is not expected to service too many nodes before it joins, not all neighbors are therefore expected to respond to the request for *Bf* recommendation. The interest here is on the cumulative *Bf* value, not the average. We pass the accumulated *Bf* through a unit step function $\Theta(Bf)$, that returns either 0 or 1 depending on the value it receives, according to equation (4.2), where n_{min} is the minimum Bf required from a newcomer.

$$\Theta(Bf) = \begin{cases} 0 & \text{if Bf} < n_{min} \\ 1 & \text{otherwise} \end{cases} \tag{4.2}$$

The self signed certificates mentioned previously, do not stop generation of multiple identities, but they do help to verify that malicious nodes do not try to impersonate existing trustworthy ones; a duplicate ID would signal a red flag. New nodes usually do some work in order to gain entry into the network, which is to service some nodes that are already in the network upto some limit. This would mean spending some resources and a bit of time by the newcomers. Since resources (including bandwidth) are not usually limitless, the number of sybils that a sybil attacker can introduce into the network would be limited. The (limited number of) sybils that make it into the network are further contained through the reputation and interaction rate checks, subsequently discussed. In our setup, sybil attackers also distribute fake blocks in the network. Their aim is not limited to selfish gain, we assume that they can also try to shutdown the network by making it hard for genuine nodes to participate.

It is important to minimize the number of admitted sybils because the lesser they are in number; the easier it would be to contain them and thus the lesser their effect. Outsourcing bandwidth may be more difficult than outsourcing computation, and so the FBit method of bootstrapping may cope better with sybil attackers who may decide to outsource puzzle computation. In addition, trust requires a fraction of time to build, not just other resources. Although it may be a small time fraction, depending on how the threshold is set, it can still contribute in reducing the effect of a malicious node who may have access to high computation resources.

In general, the existing nodes are not expected to spend significant extra resources while admitting the newcomers. This is because they simply perform normal checks which they usually do for all packets, even those from known nodes. So, there is no significant burden (due to bootstrapping) on the trustors and the network in general. Whitewashing also appears less appealing and nodes are discouraged from becoming malicious after joining the network, since it takes some effort to rejoin and nodes are regularly monitored by their neighbours.

One can argue that the newcomers may have delay in connection due to the bootstrapping process. This makes sense, but let us recall that the blocks which the new nodes receive during the bootstrapping stage would eventually make sense when they join the network and download other associated blocks. This means that they did not really waste the resources or time spent in the process. Similarly, the Bf threshold can be tuned to make sure that it does not cause significant connection delay for the newcomers.

To summarize this section, the new approach does not suffer the kind of fundamental problem [118] experienced in puzzle-based methods, which has to do with the effect of disparity in resources or computation abilities between legitimate users and would-be attackers. With the new method, even if a would-be attacker has access to large computational resources, it may not make a significant difference. Moreover, the proposed method favours productivity, because newcomers actually render valuable help, and in return gain reputation. As explained in subsection 4.4, this method can be adapted to similar other protocols. It is distributed, and was not built to depend on any seed node or super peer.

4.2 Familiarity

Many distributed protocols (especially P2P) operate in a "give and take" manner. This means that the network can be self-sustaining, without relying on a dedicated single server. The idea behind the familiarity concept is to enable nodes to ascertain how much each neighbor has contributed to them particularly, and to the network in general. We assume that more familiar nodes interact more often, and if genuine, contribute more to each other. This idea, in a sense is similar to the tit-for-tat method of BitTorrent where nodes prioritize neighbors that have given more to them.

However, unlike BitTorrent where nodes act mainly based on local tit-for-tat views, the new method allows peers to also ascertain the global impact of each node on every other node in the network (or neighbourhood) at a given time, in-terms of resource contribution, on a scale of 0 to 1. This ensures that a more liberal and reputable node, gains more advantage, not just for its reputation but also for its liberality in terms of rendering services to others.

In a nutshell, not only the reputation of a node is important, but also the rate of contribution that led to the acquisition of such reputation; this is captured by the familiarity concept. Neither reputation nor rate alone can account for optimal fairness, thus the need to combine them. We shall focus on familiarity in this section, and then capture reputation in the next.

Equation (4.3) captures the activity rate of peers in a network at intervals (t = 20 seconds). If node i downloads from node j, or uploads to it, i records an interaction (download or upload), and vice versa. We also take note of unanswered requests, because they could be signs of maliciousness, such as lying piece attack. Interaction time is also recorded. Given that node i has x successful interactions (or transactions) with node j within time t, it calculates the interaction rate of node j, $IR_{ij}(t)$ using equation (4.3);

$$IR_{ij}(t) = x_{ij}(t)/n_{max}, \qquad (4.3)$$

where n_{max} is derived by dividing the node's bandwidth by the size of each block and multiplying the result by time (t). Literally, n_{max} is the optimal rate at which each peer is expected to function in the swarm within t interval, and it is recalculated every

t seconds. An alternative way to determine n_{max} in an environment where knowing the bandwidth is difficult, would be to collect votes from nodes that have interacted with the 'newcomer', reflecting their experience and using that to estimate n_{max}. Nodes pay more attention to neighbors who service them in return. If extended, it means that nodes give to neighbors who give back to the network, in order to ensure sustainability. A successful transaction means a non-malicious upload or download.

As familiarity grows, IR tends to 1. n_{max} is chosen in a way that keeps IR below 1 within the time (t) range. However, in rare cases, and depending on the choice of n_{max}, IR can be greater than 1. When this happens, the excess is not considered, so IR simply equals 1.

As already noted, most earlier TRSs use parameters such as the difference between number of a peer's *'downloads from'* and *'uploads to'* another peer as a way of determining cooperation. For instance, if node i has uploaded z chunks to node j and downloaded y chunks from it, then y minus z will be the bases for determining the fairness or otherwise of j, from the perspective of i. In some cases, ratio is used instead of subtraction, mostly in models that are based on probability expectation value [33]. y and z can also represent the number of favourable and unfavourable interactions respectively. Unanswered requests are often counted among the unfavourable transactions.

The problem with such method is that the cumulative interaction rate does not reflect adequately on the end results. As an example, consider a case where y = 500, and z = 499, the difference will be 1, just the same as when y = 2 and z = 1, ignoring the interaction frequencies, which can be a vital factor by itself. If we take the ratio of good interactions over total, then the case with fewer interaction may be at clear advantage, which can be somewhat unjust. Wang P. et al. [119], identified similar problem, but their approach soldered the concept rigidly into trust computation, such that it might be a problem when emphasis is preferred either on just trust or frequency.

In case of high familiarity and a sudden unsatisfactory interaction, we can probe further to ascertain if the nodes were under resource strain when they malfunctioned, and also consider the severity of the unfair act they have portrayed. Such act of further probe may enable nodes to be fairer in dealing with neighbors and help them to identify some attack patterns. In a nutshell, we use this concept of familiarity to capture the activity rate of a peer, not just locally, but generally in the network, on the scale of 0 to 1. Trust score alone can hardly reveal this relationship. We have applied it more specifically in subsection 4.5 to tackle bandwidth attack.

4.3   Reputation Score Computation

Applying the concept of probability expectation value [33], and based on recorded interaction experience, non-malicious downloads are associated with α, while the bad ones plus uploads (as well as no replies) are associated with β. Expected reputation (DT_{ij}), based on the behaviour of node j, according to the direct experience of node i with respect to time (t), is given in equation (4.4).

$$DT_{ij_{(t)}} = \frac{\alpha_{ij_{(t)}} + \Theta(Bf_{i_j})}{\alpha_{ij_{(t)}} + \beta_{ij_{(t)}} + \Theta(Bf_{i_j})} \tag{4.4}$$

A download is considered non-malicious if its piece is hashed without error. If there is a mismatch in the hash code, it is considered malicious. *Bf* serves as a normalizing factor when computing expected reputation, since every node in the neighbourhood of i is expected to have been bootstrapped, which implies that it has $Bf{>}0$. In the equation, *Bf* is not time-dependent because it does not really change after the bootstrapping stage. The number of uploads counts for β because we want the reputation score to reflect credibility and at the same time uphold the tit-for-tat attribute which allows leechers to prioritize nodes that upload more contents to them. For example, free-riders who do not really circulate bad files can still get a reputation drop by their act of not giving.

As the number of interactions grows, the behaviour of nodes may change, making it important for older interactions to have less weight or be completely forgotten. After more than 1 interactions (i.e. if $\exists\ DT_{ij_{(t-1)}}$), aging factor is introduced. The aging factor used here is related to that of [8] and it basically considers the similarity between previous records and a recent outcome; the wider the difference, the less consideration such history is given. If we denote the aging factor as $\rho^{(t)}$, then we can update our local experience with respect to the most recent transaction, at time (t), with equation (4.5). This equation also applies to IR computation.

$$DT_{ij_{(t)}} = \rho^{(t)} DT_{ij_{(t-1)}} + (1 - \rho^{(t)}) DT_{ij_{(t)}} \qquad (4.5)$$

To get a general view of the reputation and participation of any neighbor, nodes usually ask others for recommendations concerning that neighbor. Replies to such recommendation requests usually come in pairs; DT and IR. Considering our testbed (modified BitTorrent), nodes can also update the tracker with recommendation information when they make contacts, although such tracker update is not a requirement for the proposed method. When a node asks for recommendation from its (good) neighbors, it ranks each recommendation according to the reputation of the recommending node, using the Ordered Weighted Average (OWA) [120]. The choice of OWA is due to its weight tuning advantage, which allows us to easily associate each indirect score with the reputation of the node that sent them. If node i asks its n sequence of neighbors j, about another peer l; i discounts collected recommendations (DT_{jl}), and Interaction Rates (IR_{jl}) as indicated in equations (4.6) and (4.7).

$$IT_{il_{(t)}} = \frac{\sum_{j=1}^{n} DT_{ij_{(t)}} \cdot DT_{jl_{(t)}}}{\sum_{j=1}^{n} DT_{ij_{(t)}}} \qquad (4.6)$$

$$CIR_{il_{(t)}} = \frac{\sum_{j=1}^{n} IR_{ij_{(t)}} \cdot IR_{jl_{(t)}}}{\sum_{j=1}^{n} IR_{ij_{(t)}}} \qquad (4.7)$$

Where $IT_{il_{(t)}}$ and $CIR_{il_{(t)}}$ are the reputation and IR of l respectively, according to i, based on the information it got from other peers. Assuming that $DT_{jl_{(t)}}$ are arranged in descending order. Similarity check which is elaborated in section 4.6, is performed on the collected recommendations before computation. This is to sieve out recommendations that may have been submitted by colluding attackers.

The trustee's score based on the the direct experience of the trustor ($DT_{il_{(t)}}$) can be added at the discounting stage, i.e. using equations (4.6) and (4.7). In that case, the trustor uses a peak score of 1 to show that it trusts itself completely. Alternatively, recommended scores (IT, CIR) and direct scores (DT, IR) can be distinct, and later merged with equations (4.8) and (4.9), adjusting the weight ($0 \leq \sigma_d \leq 1$) to suit peculiar needs. We adopted the latter (using equations (4.8) and (4.9)) for the results shown in this work, with a weight of 0.6 assigned to σ_d. In our experience, this value appears optimal because it gives trust an upper hand, without undermining the familiarity factor.

$$TR = \sigma_d \cdot DT + (1 - \sigma_d) \cdot IT, \tag{4.8}$$

$$TIR = \sigma_d \cdot IR + (1 - \sigma_d) \cdot CIR, \tag{4.9}$$

where TR stands for Total Reputation, and TIR is the Total Interaction Rate. They can further be merged with equation (4.10), to arrive at a General Score (GS). We observed on the course of this work that considering the IR factor can make a difference, compared to when it is not considered. $0 \leq \sigma_t \leq 1$ is another weighting factor used in equation (4.10); it has same value as σ_d mentioned previously.

$$GS = \sigma_t \cdot TR + (1 - \sigma_t) \cdot TIR \tag{4.10}$$

4.4   Modified BitTorrent Unchoke Algorithm for Leechers

For clarity, we have divided the algorithm into two parts. The first (Algorithm 1) briefly discussed in this section, captures the steps that FBit leechers take when unchoking other leechers. While the second part (Algorithm 2) which is presented in the next subsection, depicts the steps that seeders take when unchoking leechers. Algorithm 1 applies the earlier discussed concepts of bootstrapping, familiarity and reputation to mitigate sybil attack, fake-block attack, free-ridding, and collusion attack; while Algorithm 2 focuses specifically on stopping bandwidth attacks. The two algorithms work smoothly together.

In our setup, sybil and collusion attackers also behave as fake-block attackers while in the network. This means that in addition to their respective traditional behaviours which were earlier outlined, they distribute fake-blocks (only) when they gain access into the network. Collusion attackers know themselves and do not send fake blocks to each other, only to others.

The acronyms used in the algorithms are explained as follows:

- *MaxUnchoke*; used to indicate the maximum number of neighbors a server node can service simultaneously at a given time.

- *NumberUnchoked*; used to show the number of neighbors that is currently being served by a given node.

- *InterestedPeerList*; keeps a list of neighbors that are interested in a given block of the file.

- *TrustedPeerList*; used to keep a list of nodes (among those interested in the current block) which have reputation scores that are above *'threshold'*.

- *threshold*; minimum score (0.5) a peer must have before it can be added to the list (*'InterestedPeerList'*) of those that will be considered for a given transaction.

Algorithm 1 Leecher Unchoke Method

1: $MaxUnchoke = c$
2: $NumberUnchoked = 0$
3: $InterestedPeersList \leftarrow P$
4: $TrustedPeerList \leftarrow \{\}$
5: **while** $NumberUnchoked \leq MaxUnchoke$ **do**
6:     **for** all peers(P) in InterestedPeerList **do**
7:         Calculate IR and DT scores()
8:         **if** IR Is High **then**
9:             $TR = DT$
10:             $TIR = IR$
11:         **else**
12:             Get recommendations and check similarity
13:             Apply equations (4.6) to (4.9)
14:             Calculate GS() according to (4.10)
15:         **end if**
16:         **if** $TR \geq threshold$ **then**
17:             $TrustedPeerList \leftarrow p$
18:         **end if**
19:         Sort TrustedPeerList by GS()
20:         Unchoke Top Scores First()
21:         $NumberUnchoked + +$
22:     **end for**
23:     RemovePFromInterestedPeersList
24: **end while**

In a nutshell, here is the function of each line in the first algorithm. Lines 1 and 2 initiate *MaxUnchoke* and *NumberUnchoked* variables respectively, while lines 3 to 4 start the lists of *InterestedPeerList* and *TrustedPeerList*. According to line 5, if a node is currently able to service any additional neighbor, it selects a trustee from the *InterestedPeerList* (line 6) and calculates the IR and DT of the trustee (line 7). If the trustee is very familiar to the trustor (line 8) then scores are based on direct experience only (lines 9 and 10), otherwise recommendations are collected (lines 12) and used for calculating scores (lines 13). By skipping indirect score computation when IR is high, we can save some computation effort.

When recommendations are collected, a similarity check which is triggered by line 12 of algorithm 1, is also done. Similarity check is explained in subsection 4.6.1. GS is afterwards calculated in line 14. However, if a trustee has a TR that is below threshold, it does not qualify to be considered for any service (lines 16 to 18). Those who are qualified to receive services are serviced according to their GS scores beginning with the highest score (lines 19 and 20). When a transaction process is initialized, the trustee is removed from the *InterestedPeerList* (line 23).

When nodes are able to validate each other and complete transactions, they mutually update reputations and interaction rates, reflecting their experiences. In Algorithm 1, leechers use such updates in determining requests to respond to, and the priority that each requester deserves. Equations (4.4) and (4.3) are applied to update direct reputation and familiarity (rate) information respectively. If a node has communicated regularly with consistent reputation for a considerable amount of time (even recently), then direct/local information is sufficient for making trust decisions. This is to save resources that would otherwise be used to gather and compute recommendations. Ofcourse, local experience may be built upon recommendations that were collected at some point in the past.

Trustors contact neighbors for recommendations when they do not have enough information to assess the trustee, or when the familiarity which exists between the two nodes is not high enough. Line 13 of algorithm 1 triggers equations (4.6) to (4.9) which are responsible for computing indirect scores and combining them with direct experience of the trustor. The general score (GS) is further calculated using equation (4.10) which basically applies desired weights to merge reputation and familiarity scores. Based on the GS, all trustees that are not considered malicious are collected in a list and priority is given to each according to its contribution and reputation in the network.

4.4.1 FBit in DHT (Distributed Hash Table) Protocols

Although peers may be given different names in different platforms, the concept of seeder (service giver) and leecher (service receiver) is quite common. In most cases, network peers serve as both service providers and consumers. The algorithms presented in this work have not been built to rigidly fit into BitTorrent architecture alone. Focus has been more on the nodes, so that any similar architecture would require minimal tuning to adapt it.

DHT (including MLDHT) makes it possible for the network to function without a tracker. Every node acts as a mini tracker; they collectively perform the task of discovering other peers which are in the network. In MLDHT, nodes randomly choose 160-bit unique ID which also contains some information about their distances. At first, nodes need to query the k-bucket to know peers that are closest to the infohash. The client node further tries to connect to the closest peers in order to initiate queries. Given that the connected node is aware of the peers which are associated with the infohash, it returns a list of such peers, and file download continues similar to the way it happens in the traditional protocol [121].

Just before the download processes, the reputation bootstrapping can happen for newcomers. Key exchange messages can be embedded in any of the control messages mentioned earlier (e.g. 'FIND_NODE'), while newcomers may be served after successfully responding to requests, such as requests for peers that are associated with the infohash (which the newcomer should have at this stage). In the current implementation of the proposed system, the tracker does not perform any special task, every node is regarded as equal. This is a way of making it non-centralized and enabling its adaptability to other platforms.

FBit is focused more on content downloads (retrieval/storage) and less on routing, but it can be featured in both processes. Instead of considering only the distance while choosing the k-bucket nodes, *GS* score in FBit can be introduced into the process (as done in the next chapter). A weighted average of the *GS* and "distance factor" can be adopted, similar to the method used in [75]. With the advantages being reputation bootstrapping, computation of indirect reputation and mitigation of bandwidth attack; contrary to assigning positive risk factors to newcomers and using only direct scores, as done in [75]. This is elaborated in subsequent chapters.

Similarly, in Gnutella [122], peers perform the task of both servers and clients. To join, Gnutella newcomers connect to any known host, and through that means get in-touch with other nodes. Such known host(s) can serve as the initial trustor(s) in the bootstrapping stage of the proposed system. Similarly, the "broadcast" and "back-propagation" of information in Gnutella can serve as means of relating the reputation (and other information) of peers to other neighbours within the network.

The new method has been derived to fit into edge computing protocols, particularly the mobile edge-clouds. In most edge computing paradigms, edge elements (nodes) are usually supported by access points and occasionally by the cloud infrastructure; this may be an added advantage because they may help bring some coordination (like the tracker does), making trust computation easier. Our focus is however more on mobile edge-clouds where nodes can be completely independent, with no hierarchical communication pattern in the network.

4.5 Modified BitTorrent Unchoke Algorithm for Seeders

As mentioned earlier, malicious peers take advantage of the opening discussed under bandwidth attack to abuse seeders and download mainly from them, thereby blocking their unchoke slots (i.e. making them unable to upload to legitimate peers). Such behaviour also enable the malicious nodes to avoid downloading from other leechers who could measure their contributions based on experience.

To check this, FBit in algorithm 2 warrants that a leecher (l) who requests download from a seeder (s), has to submit its top IR information alongside its request. Seeder (s) uses such information to determine how much l has uploaded and downloaded from its fellow leechers. s then gives priority to peers that are more selfless in their services to other leechers, in order to motivate them and encourage others not to be selfish. It also mitigates a kind of denial of service attack that would occur if the unchoke slots of seeders are congested by attackers. This algorithm further holds each peer responsible for, not only its reputation, but also the impact it is able to make in the network. Recall that seeders are basically service givers who have no need for receiving. P2P networks need them and they need to be encouraged and optimally protected.

It is possible for two leechers to collude and submit false information about each other, to gain priority. However, they cannot control the information which other leechers submit about them; this may lead to information mismatch (by a high margin), giving the seeder a clue of foul play.

Algorithm 2 Seeder Unchoke Method

1: $MaxUnchoke \leftarrow \{predefined\}$
2: $InterestedPeersList \leftarrow \{\}$
3: $NumberUnchoked \leftarrow 0$
4: **while** $NumberUnchoked \leq MaxUnchoke$ **do**
5:     CollectVotesIncludingRecentlyCached()
6:     DoIntermitentScoreValidation()
7:     CountVoteForEachP()
8:     UnchokeHighestVotedP()
9:     **if** PeersHaveSameVote() **then**
10:         UnchokePWithHigherIRScore()
11:     **end if**
12:     $NumberUnchoked + +$
13:     RemovePFromInterestedPeersList()
14:     **if** VotedP Is Not In $InterestedPeersList$ **then**
15:         CacheVote()
16:     **end if**
17: **end while**

As an illustration, nodes l, i, and j in Figure 4.1 represent individual peers in a swarm who request services from a seeder node. The message accompanying their requests indicate other peers (leechers) that they have downloaded the most from, and uploaded the most to. A malicious node who chooses to download only from seeders in order to dodge assessment by fellow leechers, will have little or no "upload" information to give and thus will not be qualified to make requests. Similarly, new nodes may not be able to complete this process, they have to bootstrap instead, preferably through leechers. In the illustration, node i will be served first because it has the highest vote, before node k and then node j.

Seeders can confirm scores by validating submitted scores for consistency. For instance, it could be seen that nodes i and k have both submitted scores of each other at about same time. The download rate (DR) score which i submitted concerning k is therefore expected to match the upload rate (UP) score which node k submitted concerning i, at about that same time. Line 6 of algorithm 2 executes this check, every t seconds. Earlier methods lack in this regard; they focus mainly on protecting leechers (i.e. client nodes), and give little or no attention to the seeders (i.e. server nodes).

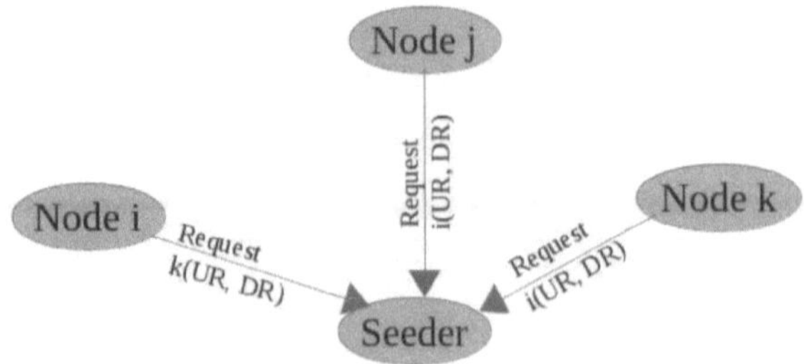

FIGURE 4.1: When Leechers Send Requests to a Seeder.

If two or more peers have the same number of votes among the submitted top leechers, then the highest IR score will be given priority, according to lines 9 to 11 of the algorithm. If their IR scores are still same, the first request will be served first. By giving priority to nodes that show more cooperation with fellow leechers, they are rewarded for being cooperative and others are encouraged to do likewise. Nodes with low score, but are genuine will have no problem downloading from other leechers in order to step up their scores. At the initial stage however, services by seeders are on first-come, first-served basis.

Seeders can also cache some of the information temporarily, so that it could be used in the near future if need be. For example, if any other node besides i, j and l were voted, its score would be cached for when such node would request a service, within the epoch (lines 14 to 16 of algorithm 2).

Here is a summary of the function of each line in algorithm 2. Lines 1 to 3 initiates the variables the same way it is done in the first algorithm, and line 4 also has similar function. Line 5 enables a server node to collect votes from its client nodes indicating the IR information of other peers which they have interacted with. The votes are then validated in line 6, while line 7 counts valid votes for each client node in the *InterestedPeerList*, and services are then rendered based on active cooperation in the network (line 8).

If the top voted peers have the same number of votes then a peer with higher IR score will be served first (lines 9 to 11). Once a transaction process is initiated, line 12 updates the number of nodes that are currently being served and line 13 removes the node from *InterestedPeerList* to indicate that it is being served. If a node is voted but has not requested for any service, its vote is cached momentarily, in-case it makes requests within the current interval. This means that calculation/validation is not necessarily done at every single request. After each transaction round, the *MaxUnchoke* is decreased.

4.6 Experiments and Results

The PeerSim simulator was used to implement a testbed for FBit. It is a java based P2P simulator which already includes a BitTorrent protocol implementation [123, 124]. This allowed us to focus on adapting the protocol to fit our use-cases.

The simulation runs on two virtual machines each with 16 CPUs at 2500MHz and 64GB RAM. Each machine runs OpenJDK Runtime Environment 1.8, and Python 3.4.3 which is used for scripting. PeerSim has a configuration file that allows parameters to be adjusted as desired. Some of such parameters include;

- *network.size*; it is used to specify the network size, and it was set to 100.

- *network.node.direct_weight*; this is a new addition, used to specify the weight of direct scores (that is IR and DT). It was set to 60 percent.

- *protocol.urt* was set to "UniformRandomTransport", which is the transport protocol used by the simulator.

- *protocol.simulation.file_size*; this is used to specify the size of the file to be shared in the network. The process is completely successful if every peer downloads a complete file before the process ends. It was set to 20mb in the simulation. This file size was used (instead of a bigger file) just to make the experiment faster, since each stage is repeated up to 30 times, before obtaining the confidence level. We however expect similar performance regardless of file size.

- *protocol.simulation.duplicated_requests*; this was set to 1, meaning that a node can only send one request for a particular block at a time. It could be set to any other value if desired. We did not study the effect of varying this parameter, but setting it to 2 for example may even make the bootstrapping process a little better. Imagine that a newcomer is malicious and refuses to forward the correct block routed through it, the existing node would simply fall back to the duplicate request, without making a fresh request for the same block.

- *init.net.seeder_number*; this was set to 1, so that each simulation begins with one seeder. There are other variables that are initialized at the start of the simulation such as the number of attackers. When a type of attack is not present, its value is set to 0 (eg. *init.net.nCollusionAttacker 0*). There are also some controls that allow us to observe and get feedback from the simulation (eg. control.observer.step simulation.logtime). During "logtime", we update the files that have been created to store needed information which is used to measure the performance of the network.

- *protocol.simulation.max_swarm_size* was set to 200 to show that the network can only grow to a maximum of 200 nodes (there is no specific reason for choosing 200, except that we needed a number that is more than the network size which is 100). This can change to accommodate any network size of choice.

- *random.seed*; every simulation needs to have a seed value. Using the scripts, this and other necessary variables are automatically generated at the beginning of each simulation. In the case of the random seed, the script generates it randomly, while other values (such as percentages of attacker) are picked accordingly from the series of provided values. Event based engine of Peersim was used for this experiment.

A 95 percent confidence level was maintained for the recorded simulation results, this is in order to statistically validate their consistency. Simulations were ran with network size of 100 nodes, and varied number of malicious nodes, to determine their impact in each case. Different attacks were simulated including sybil, fake-block and collusion attacks, with the goal of determining how efficiently such attacks are mitigated using the new bootstrapping and mitigation approach, compared to other methods. The original BitTorrent method [123] and another Trust Management System (TMS) by Sarjaz et al. [66] were adopted for comparison. For TMS, we implemented it using the information provided in [66]. TMS was chosen for comparison because it addressed similar attacks (such as fake-block attack), and was also tested on BitTorrent platform.

In TMS, each node calculates the local scores of its neighbours, and sends the scores to the tracker (a kind of central node) who determines the top 10 percent nodes, based on the scores. The top 10 percent nodes then determine the global scores of other nodes. The global scores are returned to the nodes so they can use it for decision making. Nodes can be assigned a low score if they share fake blocks for example. But the familiarity concept we discussed earlier is not accounted for, and any node can (re)join; no bootstrapping. Additionally, when a node becomes a seeder, it is no longer able to calculate local scores, leaving it potentially disadvantaged. These explain why TMS could not withstand sybil (plus fake-block) attack in this experiment.

The simulation began with a single seeder in each case, and runs until a 95 percentage confidence level is attained, and the average is taken afterwards. Each simulation can run up to 30 times. The file size is 20mb for all experiments. This work did not address the implications related to churn, nodes stay in the network throughout the simulation.

The presented results were obtained with network size 100 and varied percentages (0, 10, 20, 30, 40, and 50, 60, 70, 80) of attackers. For clarity, we once again state that what we call a sybil attacker in this context is actually both a sybil and a fake-block attacker. When the sybil attacker makes its way into the network, it also circulates fake blocks; more sybils means more fake-blocks and higher chance of shutting down the network. This is important for understanding the result.

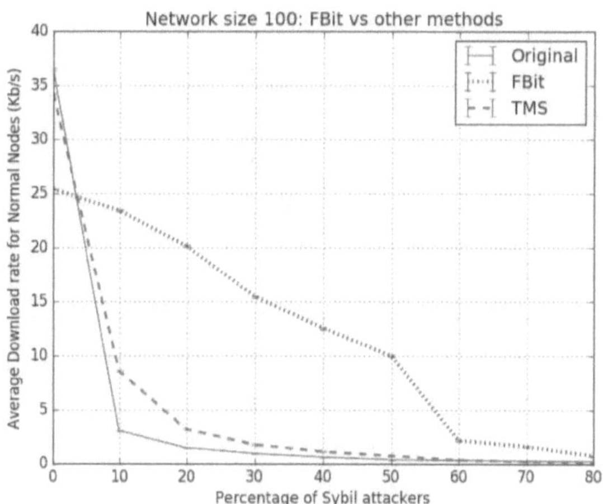

FIGURE 4.2: FBit vs other methods; showing the difference in download rate for non-malicious nodes. FBit allows them to download at higher rate amidst sybil attackers.

Figure 4.2 presents a result of how the network responded to sybil attackers, who also distribute fake-blocks when they are able to gain access. The result compares FBit to the original tit-for-tat based BitTorrent and TMS. As shown, non-malicious nodes suffered less attack with FBit compared to other methods; they are able to download at significantly faster rate. The core reasons for the improved performance center on the following: (i) sybil attackers, to a large extent, can be stopped before they enter the network and cause any disruption; (ii) for some of the attackers who make it into the network, the algorithm is also able to capture them early enough, minimizing their impact; (iii) seeders can protect themselves from exploitation. Most TRSs address the second point but not the first and third points.

The proposed bootstrapping method stops attackers at the point of entry. Introducing sybils becomes costly and an attacker can only introduce a limited number of sybils based on its capacity, knowing that it may be difficult to outsource bandwidth. Attackers that manage to enter the network are further fished out by monitoring their behaviours. The IR computation particularly protects the seeders from exploitation. If a node is found to be circulating fake blocks, it is blacklisted. Other forms of maliciousness such free-riding result in trust depreciation.

When the number of sybils rose beyond 50 percent of the network size, the graph (Figure 4.2) indicates that their effect on the FBit network became stronger, and mitigating them led to a sharp decrease in the download rate of legitimate nodes. This is expected because, with very high percentages of sybils, there will be more failed and repeated transactions. Transactions fail when nodes suspect that their neighbor is likely a sybil, and decline its offers (or refuse to engage it). When this repeats, more time will be needed to find the right nodes, and thus the overall transaction time will increase.

Also noteworthy is the fact that attackers do not upload any good block. The only resource (e.g. file) available for sharing in the network is the one that the good nodes possess. As the percentage of attackers increases, the overall resources of the network reduces, this further explains why the download rate of FBit's non-malicious nodes declined as attackers grew in number. This is also true for malicious and non-malicious nodes in the other two methods.

As briefly pointed out earlier, reputable nodes which are already in the network do not incur much cost by introducing or validating newcomers, except for slight 'transaction time trade-off' that may arise as a result of routing some chunks or queries through the newcomer. Such trade off is however compensated by the gain in reputation that the trustor stands to get after successfully introducing a new node. The delay caused by forwarding some packets (or queries) through the newcomers appears mild. Albeit, our method suffers some overhead which is clearly visible when there are no attackers (i.e. zero percent) in the network, according to Figure 4.2.

TMS could not cope with sybil attackers because of the earlier mentioned flaw in the bootstrapping method. If sybils can be introduced almost at no cost, an attacker can easily introduce many of them and hijack the network at early stage. In tit-for-tat, new comers are admitted without checks via optimistic unchoke, giving room for attackers who sap the available resources and frustrates the network with fake blocks.

In another round of experiment, FBit was exposed to collusion attacks, where fake-block attackers cooperate to favour themselves, and downgrade the reputation of others that are not in their clique. Figure 4.3 captures the performance of FBit in comparison with tit-for-tat based BitTorrent and TMS. A careful look at the result reveals that FBit can cope with collusion attacks. Although collusion attackers appear to have higher impact compared to a non collusion scenario such as figure 4.2, FBit nodes are still able to download at considerably fair rate. The noticed decline in download rate (with higher percentage of attackers) is expected, because finding reliable nodes becomes more difficult and more time consuming. The TMS method felt more collusion impact, while the original method was completely overwhelmed.

Similar to the sybil attackers explained earlier, in addition to the traditional behaviour of collusion attackers, they also exhibit the characteristics of fake-block attackers. The nodes collude and distribute fake blocks to other (good) nodes that are not in their clique. The goal of the attackers is beyond selfish gain, the assumption is that they may also want to shutdown the network, and this is achieved when genuine nodes are unable to download. They also indirectly exhibit bandwidth attack attributes, since seeders are more likely to become victims if they lack information to make decisions, like the leechers.

To guard against collusion attack, TMS uses recommendations from top 10 nodes to compute the score of the other peers. From the result, this does not appear effective because malicious nodes also stand the chance of joining the top nodes, especially with exaggerated scores from other colluding nodes. Tit-for-tat also does not combat collusion attack and nodes may be overwhelmed by malicious traffic from the attackers. For example they can be trapped in a cycle of downloading, verifying and discarding fake blocks; making it impossible for them to successfully complete transactions. Moreover,

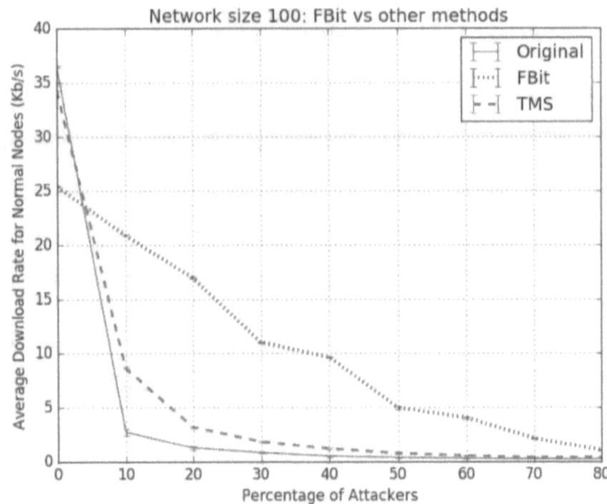

FIGURE 4.3: Collusion Attack.

in TMS and the original method, attackers are able to steal resources from seeders. FBit copes with collusion attack using similarity check which is explained shortly (in subsection 4.6.1).

To measure how successful an attack is, we compared how the malicious nodes fared with the performance of the non-malicious ones. Ideally, non-malicious nodes are expected to beat the attackers and maintain a clearly higher download rate. Figure 4.4 illustrates this, with non-malicious nodes downloading clearly at higher rates in FBit, while the collusion attackers were dominating in the other methods. The gap is more in the original method and less in TMS, indicating that TMS is more resilient to collusion attack than the original method.

A Resilient system is expected to frustrate attackers and allow non-malicious nodes to download faster. In the original and TMS methods, attackers are able to download, especially from seeders. TMS performed better than the original method, but was still tricked by the attackers. FBit is clearly more successful in stopping the attackers from stealing resources, showing resilience against bandwidth attack which the seeders are often exposed to. In this way, the network resources are conserved, ensuring that it does not shut down. Although Figure 4.4c appears to show that the malicious nodes in FBit downloaded zero blocks, the value is not exactly zero, but rather very small. This

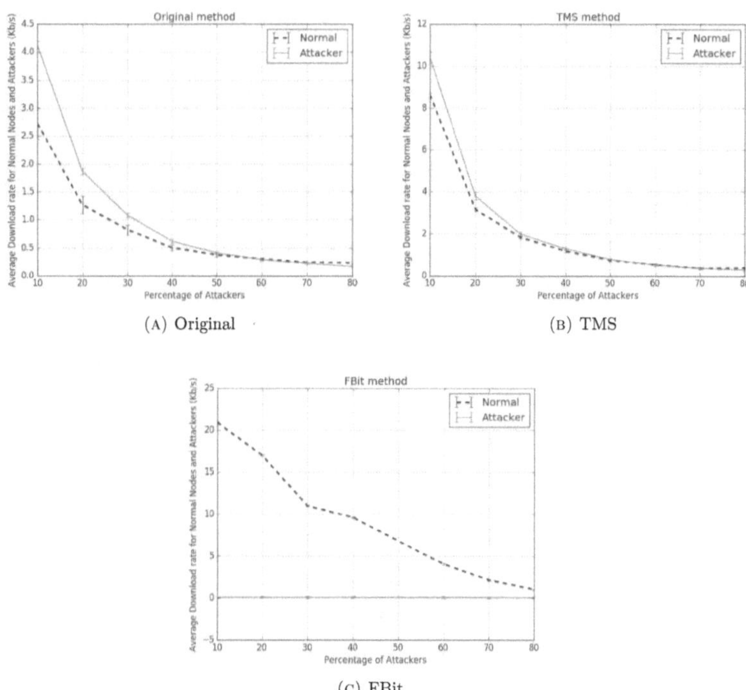

FIGURE 4.4: The download rate of genuine nodes versus attackers in the (a) original, (b) TMS and (c) FBit methods.

does not necessarily mean that no attacker entered the network, it simply means that the good nodes, with the help of the algorithm, is able to avoid downloading from, and uploading to, the attackers. Nonetheless, the bootstrapping method makes the process easier by stopping most sybils from getting into the network. The overhead incurred in the process by FBit is already shown in Figure 4.3.

4.6.1 Similarity Check

Before we summarize this chapter, let us discuss the similarity check which was mentioned earlier.

Some models have applied neighbor similarity to detect attackers in a distributed protocol. For example, in [125], if recommendations collected from various nodes regarding a peer is significantly divergent (not similar) then such peer would raise suspicion. Their approach was designed for e-commerce, and it requires coordination from some form of central agents such as group leaders, which can be a limitation. However, we tapped from their idea of similarity, and applied it (with modifications) to tackle collusion attack.

In FBit, when a peer is sending a request for recommendation, it selects some trusted neighbor(s) randomly from its neighbor list, and sends request for recommendation regarding the selected nodes and the actual unfamiliar node (i.e. the would-be collusion attacker). So, the trustor requests recommendation for the actual unfamiliar peer, and at least one familiar fellow that would be used to judge the similarity between the trustor (who is requesting recommendation) and its neighbor (from whom recommendation is sought). The selected neighbour(s) must be different from the node being inquired about, and the one from whom recommendation is sought.

If the recommendation giver is in a collusion clique with the unfamiliar peer, then it will give it high score and downgrade the reputable one. Or in an attempt to mask its acts, the attacker may decide to simply exaggerate or downgrade both scores, but this would still be noticed in the similarity check. When recommendations from various neighbors are gathered, priority is given to the ones with the most similarity, based on the known peers that have been inquired about. Line 12 of algorithm 1 triggers the similarity check.

"Most similarity" here refers to the recommendations that are closest to the trust scores which the trustor has recorded regarding the familiar nodes that were included in the recommendation request. For example, if the familiar nodes are clearly downgraded while the unfamiliar one(s) has a very high score, then it may mean that the unfamiliar node is in a collusion clique with the recommendation giver.

4.7 Summary

In this chapter, the FBit algorithm was derived. "Familiarity" and reputation are among the the key ingredients required to build trust. The concept of familiarity was captured by monitoring the activity-rate of every peer locally and globally, while reputation is tracked by monitoring neighbours' behaviours directly and indirectly. The algorithm was tested on a distributed file sharing platform adapted to reflect key attributes of mobile edge-clouds. These attributes are illustrated by the use-cases discussed in the next chapter. During the test, the functionality of the tracker was drastically reduced and nodes are enabled to monitor and make their own trust and security decisions. This is to reflect a case where there is limited (or no) infrastructural support in mobile edge-clouds' network. Results obtained show that FBit can effectively avert popular attacks. We gave hints on how the system would function in other distributed scenarios, and shall elaborate on this in subsequent chapters.

Bear in mind that not every single malicious behaviour has been covered in this experiment. We focused on sybil and collusion attacks with a blend of bandwidth and fake-block attacks, in hope that it would be easy to adapt the method for similar threats. Also, FBit was derived to be able to stop other malicious behaviour such as free-riding and lying piece attack.

Chapter 5

FBit in Specific Use-cases of Mobile Edge-Clouds

FBit aims to function in both the relatively older distributed protocols and the emerging ones. It is expected to effectively feature in emerging technologies including edge computing and related paradigms. Some of these technologies have been discussed in the previous chapters including mobile edge-clouds, which is of particular interest in this work. In this chapter, we highlight some use-cases [61] of mobile edge-clouds, to further illustrate how FBit fits into them. Most of the use-cases are in line with the objectives of Hyrax project [126], which is aimed at deriving platforms for innovative applications, based on mobile edge-clouds. The book has been developed under the Hyrax project. We have specifically illustrated and tested how mobile edge-clouds would improve qual-ity of service in IoT based eHealth system, as well as the role of FBit in ensuring security in such volatile environment.

5.1 Some use-cases of Mobile edge-clouds

5.1.1 User Generated Replay (UGR)

Traditional infrastructure (e.g. WiFi) can experience enormous strain in crowded venues, such as sports arenas. Consider a football stadium for example, where an important match is taking place; thousands of people often gather to witness the competition.

Some people may be closer to an important highlight at a given time, and they would take videos and pictures of the highlights to share with other people within the sports arena. Numerous messages of that form flow through the infrastructure, dragging it to a near breaking point.

Under the concept of mobile edge-clouds, near-by devices can come together to form a pool as illustrated in figure 5.1. Contents (e.g. videos, files and photos) which are generated by the users can then be circulated in the crowd without involving any infrastructure, except as last resort. This option is faster and cheaper, and may substantially improve availability, since there is no single point of failure.

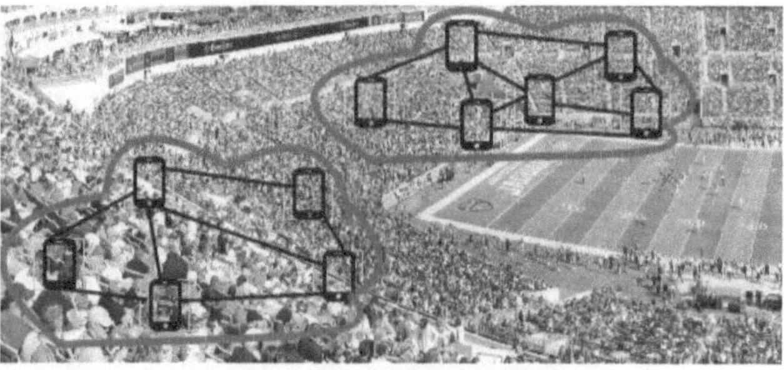

FIGURE 5.1: Sharing videos and photos in crowded venues

This use case matches the information sharing experiment which was presented in the previous chapter. FBit plays a crucial role in ensuring that nodes who may cease the opportunity to circulate unlawful or harmful contents are discovered and ejected from the mobile edge-clouds' network.

5.1.2 Rescue Assistance in Cases of Emergency

In a case of natural disaster for example, communication infrastructure which would normally be used by victims and the rescue team may be affected, and communication would be very hard or impossible. Rescue assistance systems which are designed to depend on such infrastructure also become useless once they can no longer connect.

The concept of mobile edge-clouds can help to close such gap, by enabling users within that area to connect with each other in a P2P fashion, thereby forming a network that does not rely on the infrastructure (figure 5.2). Useful information such as videos, pictures, texts, and location information may be shared within the edge-cloud network, helping the rescue team to locate people with ease.

However, individuals may find it easier to use the system if they have some confidence that there are no rogue nodes who are trying to exploit them and steal their information. FBit can help to alleviate such worry and reluctance, by ensuring that only actual nodes are connected, and that information misuse is checked by examining and observing the reputation of each connected entity. It is possible that sufficient trust may have been built during some interactions that occurred prior to the emergency, enabling nodes to have reasonable information that would help them to make safe(r) decisions. Safety remains the primary objective, which means that the new feature can be turned off, if the node is running short of energy or similar resources. If on the other hand a node has energy and other resources that is estimated to be sufficient for it to operate until rescue arrives, then the proposed system can be beneficial during and after the emergency situation.

FIGURE 5.2: Communication to aid rescue of victims in disaster scenario

5.1.3 Search for Missing Persons

Leveraging computer vision and mobile edge-clouds, face recognition can be done without relying on the cloud computing infrastructure [61] which are often remote in nature. Photos of missing persons can be searched locally on mobile devices (figure 5.3), gathering relevant information with respect to time and other factors, which would help to locate the missing person(s). Since some people are often concerned about the privacy of their data that are residing in traditional cloud infrastructure, this may be an alternative.

Additionally, it may be faster due to reduced latency, and cheaper because it may just use the idle resources of the devices involved. If need be, the edge-clouds network can also engage near-by infrastructure or the cloud.

Security would however be an issue due to lack of coordination; which on the other hand does not lack in traditional computing cloud systems. FBit is designed to close this gap by giving each device the ability to regulate access, based on reputation and cooperation; judging from its local view as well as the global view of the edge-clouds' network, as earlier outlined.

FIGURE 5.3: Search for missing person(s)

5.1.4 IoT based eHealth System:

Internet of Things (IoT) enables the connection of variety of things, including humans, animals, computers, mobile devices, sensors, software and hardware, to bring about convenient communication and improved QoS. An IoT platform is primarily made up of sensors, the cloud and communication interfaces, as well as suitable algorithms.

In the context of e-Health, wearable devices with sensors are used to collect patients' data, such as heartbeat and glucose level. The data can be further processed at nearby node(s) or the cloud, depending on the network architecture. This provides a platform to monitor patients' health in real time. It enables patients to make better health decisions, e.g. about diet and exercise, while at the same time enabling doctors to, for example, determine when a patient is due for next appointment, and whether (or not) the patient is complying with prescription advice.

Architecture for IoT Based e-Health: As shown in Figure 5.4, there are four layers in the IoT based e-health architecture [127], namely; the interface, service, networking, and sensing layers. At the sensor layer, information is gathered from patients concerning their health status, and through the network layer, the gathered information can be sent to a fog node or cloud for processing. Actual e-Health service is provided at the service layer; where information is compiled and analyzed to determine the health status of patients at a given time. Result is then communicated to doctors and patients via the interface.

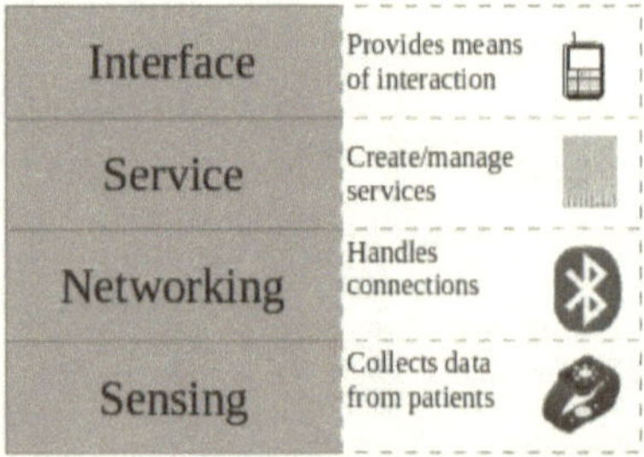

FIGURE 5.4: Architecture for IoT Based e-Health

The advantages of IoT based e-Health are clear; ranging from reduced cost, and less waiting time at hospitals, to more doctors' involvement, through real-time monitoring of patients' health status, even from a distance. Edge computing is a crucial driver of IoT, and e-Health by extension. As earlier noted, it minimizes latency and ensures optimal quality of service. Fog computing is already popular in the e-Health [128] domain. Fog nodes serve as intermediaries, placed between the edge devices and the cloud, for quicker data collection (and processing). See Figure 5.5.

Mobile Edge-clouds in e-Health: As cities and homes become smarter, the number of (e-Health) connecting devices would increase drastically; people and things would be

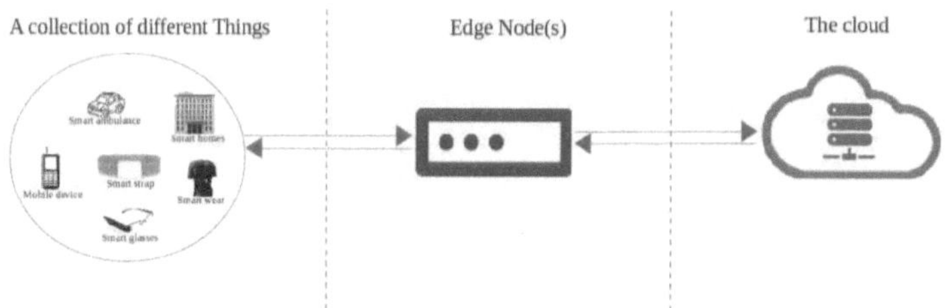

FIGURE 5.5: Simplified Architecture for IoT Based e-Health, with Fog Computing

connected on the go, via wearable, sensors, etc. This further means that there would be increased pressure on the edge nodes. To maintain a low latency e-Health system, the number of fog nodes may need to increase. The fog nodes may also need to be made more resourceful, so that they can handle more requests: these would clearly require extra infrastructural cost. In addition, fog nodes may be damaged in cases of natural disaster, cutting off people who are in the affected area, and making both e-health services and rescue operation very difficult.

Minding the crucial nature of e-Health services, mobile edge-clouds, though not popular at the moment in the e-Health domain, may be employed towards ensuring non-stop e-Health services and to aid rescue operations in cases of natural disaster. Figure 5.6 gives an illustration of how mobile edge-clouds can coexist with fog nodes, for enhanced QoS and uninterruptible e-Health service delivery. Peers no longer need to channel every traffic through a fog node at all times; this in a way tends to flatten the hierarchical communication setup of fog computing.

Fog nodes are more likely to be affected by (natural) disasters because they are often dependent on external power sources and mostly rely on established infrastructure to function. Peers that are in close proximity can pool their resources together to form edge-clouds which may be capable of addressing some requests that are within their resource limits, and offloading bulky tasks to fog nodes or the cloud. In practice, even the fog nodes can be part of a nearby mobile edge-clouds.

Some Security Issues Associated with e-Health: The attacks which were outlined earlier in this work also apply to IoT based e-Health. But the following are specific to the system, and thus worth mentioning.

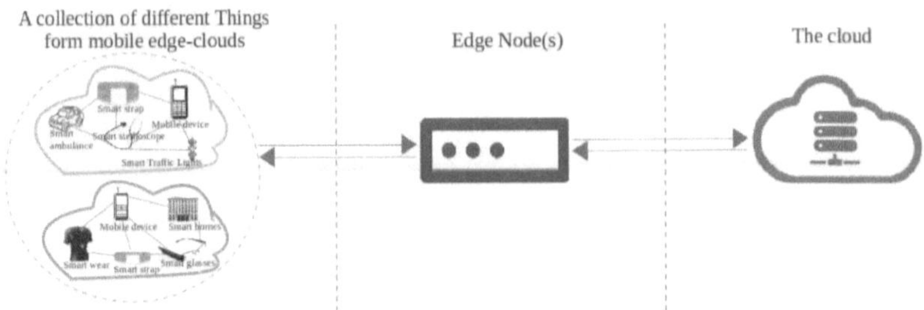

FIGURE 5.6: IoT Based e-Health, with Mobile edge-clouds

- Attack on EWS: The IoT-based Early Warning Score (EWS) can be used in e-Health to predict urgency in patients' health conditions. Very high amount of data is being generated regularly, which is too much for the medical officials and doctors to directly monitor [127]. EWS therefore helps by doing that automatically and then communicates any warning to the concerned individuals or officials. If data packets are maliciously modified, the analysis would be wrong and the process would be damaged. Similar attacks on the prescription system, hospital visit schedules, and smart ambulance can be very dangerous.

- Physical interference: Apart from the risk of modifying packets, patients can be vulnerable and easy to manipulate. This means that there may be increased risk of physical interference with the e-Health nodes/devices. Physical security for all the relevant nodes may be expensive. As a backup plan, the proposed method may help nodes to detect when its neighbour is compromised or malfunctions, and in such cases pay less attention to (or double check) information that are coming from the neighbour. The malfunctioning nodes can also be flagged.

The new method would serve as an inexpensive (extra) layer of security, and not a replacement of other security methods, such as authentication. Moreover, it is possible to steal authentication details and instantly compromise connected systems, but that would not apply to trust-based security, because time may also be required to gain reputation and become influential enough.

5.1.4.1   F-BETH

This is a modified version of FBit which targets the e-Health potential use-case, it stands for "Fairer Bits in E-healTH". F-BETH processes start with reputation bootstrapping as earlier described in Section 4.1, and Equations 4.1 and 4.2 are used to determine when nodes are able to join fully. The processes are illustrated in Algorithm 3. The goal here is to have an inexpensive means of maintaining trust and security in a kind of e-Health use-case presented earlier. It involves a mobile edge-clouds' environment which can be self-sustaining in case of emergency and can also be used in non-emergency situations where it is considered optimal, e.g. to improve QoS.

Bootstrapping may have happened before the emergency situation, since that system can also be used in non-emergency cases. Alternatively, the bootstrap threshold can be set to low if it needs to be used in an emergency, provided it is safe to do so. A node is expected to bypass F-BETH if there is an emergency and its energy (or similar resources) is running down. In that case, it does not care about trust and security - it simply connects to any available node(s), hoping for the best. This ensures that the node's safety is prioritized.

After joining the network however, nodes monitor their neighbours as they do in FBit, but mainly the reputation factor, and not the interaction rate (IR). As already emphasised, the IR information was necessary because among other things, it protects the seeders from exploitation. It is necessary in the other use-cases but less relevant for the e-Health use-case, because the network is not just for file sharing, and nodes are less likely to become dedicated seeders.

The IR factor is minimized in FBit to arrive at F-BETH. The implication is that interaction rate (in-terms of give and take) is given less attention, while more emphasis is on reputation (DT and IT). The impact of paying less attention to the IR factor was not really tested, since fairness-related behaviours including free-riding and bandwidth attacks were also left out. The goal is to illustrate the potential application of FBit in this type of environment. A non-modified version would also fit in, but resources would be spent doing computations that are not really needed. Modified BitTorrent protocol was also used for the experiment, and the tracker has similar reduced functionality; representing a fog node in this case. This simplified version may however not be so efficient in normal Bittorent protocol or the user generated replay which was mentioned earlier. The reason is that those mainly involve file sharing, and seeders may be exposed if F-BETH is used instead of FBit.

With these changes, the F-BETH algorithm is as follows:

Algorithm 3 Leecher Unchoke Method

1: $MaxUnchoke = c$
2: $NumberUnchoked = 0$
3: $InterestedPeersList \leftarrow P$
4: $TrustedPeerList \leftarrow \{\}$
5: **while** $NumberUnchoked \leq MaxUnchoke$ **do**
6:     **for** all peers(P) in InterestedPeerList **do**
7:         Calculate DT score()
8:         **if** DT Is High **then**
9:           $TR = DT$
10:         **else**
11:           Get recommendations and check similarity
12:           Calculate TR (eqn 4.8)
13:         **end if**
14:         **if** $TR \geq threshold$ **then**
15:           $TrustedPeerList \leftarrow p$
16:         **end if**
17:         Sort TrustedPeerList by TR
18:         Unchoke Top Scores First()
19:         $NumberUnchoked + +$
20:     **end for**
21:     RemovePFromInterestedPeersList
22: **end while**

The parameters are still the same as in algorithm 1, presented in the previous chapter. Equation (4.4) was still used to calculate direct trust, while (4.6) was used for indirect trust. Equations (4.5) and (4.8) were used to capture aging factor, and to combine direct and indirect trust respectively.

As expected, the results were similar to FBit's, but with some differences. As shown in Figure 5.7, the 'download' rate appears significantly better (in this experiment) for F-BETH, and slightly for the other algorithms, compared to the earlier experiments with F-Bit. Download in this context represents successfully getting replies for requested packets (and/or successful routing). Apart from difference in network conditions, arising from the fact that different random seeds were used, there are two core reasons for the noticed performance difference: (a) Because the network size is bigger in this experiment (200 nodes - double the size used in FBit experiments earlier), there are usually more reputable nodes in the network, even with similar percentages of attackers. This means that relatively more good contents are always available and thus better chances of getting them. (b) In addition, and particularly for F-BETH, less work was required during trust computation, given that IR was not computed.

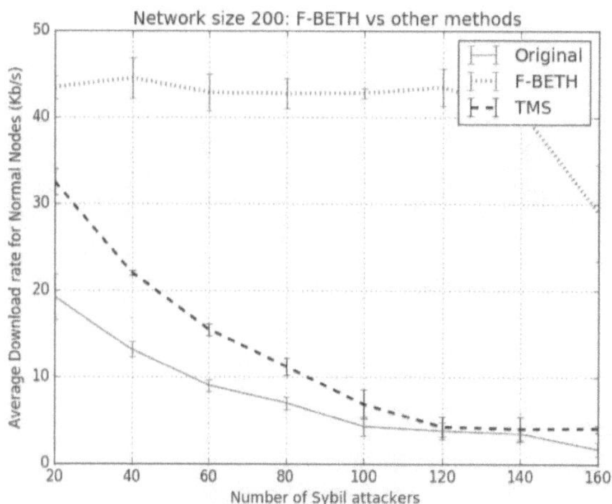

FIGURE 5.7: Download rate for normal nodes in a network of 200 nodes and varied percentage of attackers. The numbers (20, 40, 60, 80, 100, 120, 140, 160) represent actual number of attackers, equivalent to 10% to 80% of the network size.

The bootstrapping procedure remained effective, as attackers were largely stopped from joining the F-BETH (5.8c) network or circulating malicious contents. As shown in Figures 5.8, the case is not the same for TMS (5.8b) and the original (5.8a) methods, which allowed attackers to engage the resources of well behaving nodes; a situation that can give the attackers leverage to drain their resources. With focus mainly on "leechers", it makes sense that tit-for-tat (original method) appeared to perform a little better in this scenario than in the previous one, since a node attends to those that render services in return. Although the optimistic unchoke option also means that attackers may still be serviced regularly. In TMS, the attackers appear able to manipulate the trust system, thereby appearing trustworthy and receiving some services. This suggests that it may not be best fit for less hierarchical systems like this.

The overhead is expected to be similar to FBit's (see Figure 4.2), so it was not re-assessed. Also, the sybil attackers maintained similar behaviors as described earlier; they reply with bogus packets, in addition to the tradition sybil attack behaviours. Figure 5.8 illustrates how much attackers are able to get good contents or sincere services from the network versus how much genuine nodes are able to. This gives us an idea of how much the network is able to conserve its resources (e.g. energy and bandwidth) which also relates to how sustainable the network may be.

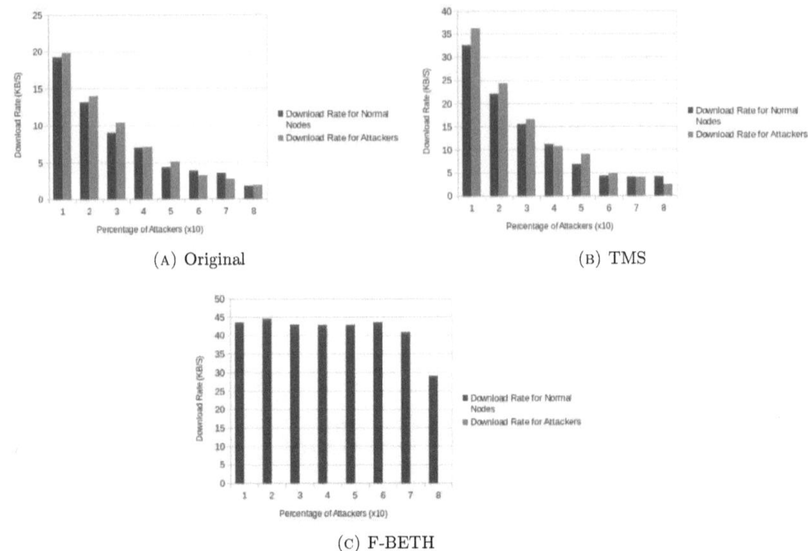

(A) Original   (B) TMS

(C) F-BETH

FIGURE 5.8: Attackers were able to access and engage the resources of their victims in other methods, but F-BETH proved effective.

Some valid questions may come to mind regarding this IoT-based e-Health use-case. For example, one may ask if it is really necessary to engage mobile edge-clouds; **is fog computing not sufficient?**

To address this, we acknowledge that fog is quite popular and in many cases it is sufficient. However, it has been found to be hierarchical in nature; participating nodes follow some hierarchy as they communicate - from IoT devices to fog (or edge) nodes, and if need be, to the cloud. While this results to improved quality of service and user experience compared to just relying on the cloud, enabling nodes to establish customized connection among themselves without always relying on the hierarchical pattern, may lead to even better performance because latency and bandwidth may be better featured. The network can also become more self-sustaining and able to better withstand disruptions. We are not alone in this line of thought, Karagiannis et al. [129] also highlighted the need for a less hierarchical approach. Mobile edge-clouds can therefore work with fog, making it possible to establish non-hierarchical connections when necessary.

Another doubt may be, **why would anyone care about security or trust in emergency scenarios?** This is clearly a valid question, and we would like to clarify that the proposed system can be bypassed in critical cases; victims can priorities survival if for example they are running out of power or other relevant resources. However, in some cases, a victim may have power and other resources that would last beyond the estimated rescue arrival time. Given such 'luxury', the victim may choose to interact only with trusted agents to guarantee security within and after the crisis. Secondly, if a node already built some trust with neighbours before the crisis (e.g. during occasional interactions) it may help it maximize its resources during the crisis by focusing on legitimate/trusted nodes who are more likely going to forward its packets, while avoiding malicious nodes that would simply drop them.

5.2   Summary

In this chapter, we have explained some use-cases of mobile edge-clouds upon which we based our study. They are in conformity with the objectives of Hyrax project, under which we worked. FBit was adapted for IoT based e-Health system. Although each edge computing paradigm has its unique flavour, it may be possible to have a blend in the future, where two or more paradigms would work together to boost availability and user experience, especially as cities become more smart and IoT-based. We presented a possible blend of mobile edge-clouds and fog computing, leveraging the attributes of mobile edge-clouds to minimize the hierarchical communication pattern of fog computing. This may enable the network to withstand emergency situations that may make traditional infrastructures unavailable; the nodes can reorganise to form a local cloud. As highlighted in the chapter, the hierarchical pattern has been viewed as potentially deficient. FBit has been weighed for application in such distributed and sensitive environment, and experimental results indicate suitability.

Chapter 6

FBit in DHT and BlockChain

In this chapter, we shall be discussing another flavour of FBit which is partly a work in progress. It has not been fully completed and tested as at the time of writing the book. We have also outlined in more detail how FBit functions with DHT (Distributed Hash Table).

6.1   FBit in DHT

To find a desired content in an unstructured P2P network, nodes broadcast their search to find as many nodes as possible, who share that content. If the content is popular, it would be easy to find, but if not, it can be problematic. The flooding technique used in the search is inefficient because it affects performance. Structured P2P solves this problem while remaining distributed, via the use of DHT. A more efficient mechanism is used to locate data by searching for nodes who have them, or are closer to their loca-tion. Although FBit has the potential to function in both structured and unstructured networks, we have focused on the former in this section, due to its advantages over the unstructured.

We have opted to implement a flavour of FBit on a Vuze client because of the similarities that exist between Vuze and some of the target use cases of mobile edge-clouds, already discussed. In addition, like in previous experiments, we seek to build on an already established protocol with known behaviour. Simulations were earlier done with respect to some of the use-cases (particularly, content sharing and IoT based e-Health) and results presented. The intention here is to setup a test-bed that would be made up of containers, which are more realistic hosts, compared to the previous simulations nodes. We have also seized the opportunity to explain (in more detail) how FBit fits into DHT based protocols. We shall highlight the functionalities of the Vuze client and other components of the test-bed as follows:

6.1.1   Vuze protocol

Kademlia is a popular DHT which is implemented in many decentralized protocols. It has two implementations; Mainline DHT and Vuze DHT - we have focused on the latter. A content description in Vuze contains an infohash, including information about leechers, seeders, torrent name and size [130]. To search for contents, a node needs to select 20 peers from its list of neighbours, and then contact them according to their proximity to the content of interest. The proximity is based on network coordinates, and each peer is responsible for calculating its network coordinates. The difference in the coordinates translates to the amount of latency that would result from a communication between the two points.

Each peer has a unique ID of 160 bits; which is a hash of the IP and port. Vuze's routing table is made up of buckets, with each bucket having about 20 nodes, identified by their IDs. An XOR of two IDs gives information about the distance between them. Usually, Kademlia nodes discover new peers and update their state using controls such as 'PING' - used to check availability, and 'findNode' and 'findValue' - used for maintaining the routing table and to discover contents respectively. Upon receiving a reply, the K-bucket is updated accordingly. Nodes may be replaced if they fail to respond to messages/control.

A Vuze node can query up to 5 peers at a time. To choose these five peers, a bucket of closest neighbours is first chosen based on the XOR distance of the IDs. The bucket nodes are sorted according to how close they are to the target. The first 10 nodes are further sorted according to the Vivaldi distance [131] of the coordinate space; this is done in order to increase lookup and reply speed. Afterwards, requests are sent to 5 top nodes. Based on the reply of those requests, discovered nodes are added and re-sorted. Unless a timeout is reached or there is no new node discovered, the process is repeated until the desired target is found [131]. For a Vuze peer to discover other nodes in the network, it needs to send messages to known nodes.

6.1.1.1 Choke and unchoke in Vuze

Peers in the network download contents and also upload same to their neighbours, unless they are free-riders. When a peer gets all the file pieces, it becomes a seeder. A file is usually divided into pieces, and then shared in a random fashion among agents in the network, applying some techniques to ensure that every piece is retained in the network as long as necessary. We shall be using the terms 'downloaders' and 'leechers' to mean the same thing.

To unchoke a node means a promise to send data to that node. Peers unchoke the fastest uploading nodes, and choke the worst uploaders. Node x shows interest in a content it wants to download from a connection via an interest message. When the connection gets such message, it checks for uploads that it has got from node x, similar to tit-for-tat mentioned previously. This is to enable it to determine whether it would send the requested packet or otherwise. Peers choose other nodes who they can serve at a given time and then choke the rest. Data pieces can be verified via the hash information which is contained in the torrent file. Every received piece is checked based on this hash, and if there is a mismatch, such piece is dropped.

The techniques used in Vuze which involves unchoking the fastest uploaders can discourage free-riding to an extent. But there are no techniques to prevent more serious attacks such as Sybil, collusion, and bandwidth attacks.

6.1.2 FBit-U

This flavour of FBit is termed FBit-U, the U stands for 'Uncontrolled' and it is used to capture the fact that we want to reflect real hosts and network behaviours as much as possible, since it would be very expensive to buy so many physical devices for experiments. It is a containerized sandbox which may also be used for similar other experiments, beyond FBit.

When a newcomer requests to join the network (through a known peer), he gets a reply through which it is able to choose its initial bucket nodes. But to actually get any content from the network, the newcomer is required to bootstrap its trust by servicing other nodes genuinely, based on the information it already has. For example, it needs to correctly reply some routing messages, to gain initial trust. Preferably, the newcomers are used to route data packets, as one of the ways to help them gain initial trust, and they are expected to deliver the data unadulterated. This is similar to the method in FBit, except that the kind of 'messages' which the newcomer routes here may be different. Nonetheless, packets which are routed through the newcomers are still expected to be intangible pieces, which the newcomer may not be able to reconstruct since it may not have all the required pieces. The overlay topology largely follows its normal pattern, the key different is that we factor in trust while choosing the neighbours, instead of just distance.

The same equation (4.1) can be used to determine when new nodes are due to join the network fully. The delay or overhead that would arise as a result of this is expected to be reasonable, following our earlier results (see figure 4.2). Nodes discover and update their buckets based on distance, as in traditional Vuze, but in addition, it is also based on trust scores of the peers. Similar to the method used in [75], the following formulae (6.1) is used to select the nodes that would make up the bucket:

$$NC = (1 - \sigma).\frac{1}{GS} + OC.\sigma, \tag{6.1}$$

where NC stands for the new closeness, GS is the trust score, OC represents old closeness which is used in traditional Vuze, and σ is the weighting factor. This is one of the significant additions made to FBit-U, most other processes work very much like in FBit, since distributed protocols has been the target from the beginning. The advantages of FBit-U over other methods such as [75] were highlighted in section 4.4.1. The inverse of GS is used in equation 6.1 because we want more trust to translate to less distance. The maximum trust score which a node can have is 1.

To calculate the trust score (GS) of any peer, reputation and rate of interaction are usually among the key factors considered, and they are calculated using the equations which were outlined earlier (4.3 to 4.10), the algorithms are also similar. In the next subsection, we will explain the experimental setup and when necessary mention some more variations between FBit and FBit-U.

6.1.3 Experiment

Apart from the first few nodes that are considered the initiators of the network, every other node is expected to go through the bootstrapping process that was outlined; no default score is assumed or assigned, and no puzzle or pre-existing trust is required. The bootstrapping procedure utilizes an already existing feature in Vuze, which allows a peer to (sometimes) send data to another node who then sends it to (you) the requester[1].

Furthermore, the traditional choke/unchoke method was also altered. Instead of focusing mainly on the number of uploads during unchoke processes, the new algorithm also considers the reputation of peers in addition to their interaction rate. We check the local and global engagement of a peer in the network; more commitment attracts higher priority. This is similar but different from the share ratio concept already existing in Vuze. Share ratio does not really account for the overall commitment of a peer in the network. It only reflects the ratio, not the total. For example, a given node who has small but equal amount of downloads and uploads, may end up with same ratio as another node who has high but also equal amount of uploads and downloads. The new system closes such gap to ensure improved fairness, as required in the use-cases.

When a seeder is seeding in the traditional Vuze client, it tends to upload to peers with the largest portion of the file[1]. In FBit-U, seeders use the IR information to check how each requester has contributed to its fellow leechers and the network in general. This protects the seeders from abuse and bandwidth attack.

Modifications were also made to allow a form of authentication of nodes. At the initial stage of the new system, nodes send their self-signed certificate to an existing node through which they wish to join. That is then associated with the newcomer and further spreads through the network so that members can use it to verify its signature. FBit-U pieces are signed using elliptic curve digital signature algorithm, and are verified by the recipients. The behaviours of malicious nodes were also implemented, including fake-block, bandwidth, collusion, and sybil attacks.

---

[1]https://wiki.vuze.com/w/This_funny_word#Unchoking (accessed 11/04/2019).

We also used gRPC [2]. to build a control module that allows us to control the experiment. With this, we could issue commands to all nodes at the same time and also collect required logs. gRPC is explained in the next subsection.

6.1.4 Components of the test-bed

- Vuze: this is already discussed in the previous subsection. It forms a basic framework upon which modifications are made to attain the desired platform for testing the new system. The bootstrapping mechanism is to be implemented here, as well as the trust model. At the time of joining the network, nodes choose a public and private key pair (K_p, K_b). The new node notes the private key and sends a self signed certificate alongside a request to join the network.

  When an existing node receives the request, it associates the public key with that new node, if it does not exist already. It further requests that some of its packets be forwarded through the newcomer who it wishes to introduce into the network; this would give the newcomer some initial reputation if routed correctly. The process would be repeated by the same existing node or alongside other nodes to make the process faster. Newcomers join the network after meeting an entry threshold which is normalized so that it does not impose too much burden on them.

  After gaining full entry into the network, bootstrap process is considered to be complete for that node. The interaction rate and reputation of the new node is continually monitored by its neighbours. The process involved in doing this is same as outlined in the previous chapters. Equation 4.3 is used to calculate the interaction rate, also called the familiarity rate, while Equation 4.4 is used to monitor the reputation based on direct experience.

  To make a node's familiarity and reputation spread throughout the network, recommendation is used; this involves nodes asking about the trust of other nodes (which they are not very familiar with) before completing interactions with them. Priority is given to nodes with higher commitment and reputation, and this is calculated using Equations 4.6 and 4.7. Equations 4.8 to 4.10 are used to combine the scores into a single trust score which represents how much the network trusts a given peer.

---

[2]https://grpc.io/docs/guides/concepts/ (accessed 29/05/2019).

Every node is independent, and only needs to participate and interact correctly with its neighbours; this is suitable for a fully distributed environment which we envisage. It is also applicable to partially distributed setups. The use of signatures and unique keys minimizes the chances of fake identities, while the bootstrapping exercise further helps to keep Sybil attack and similar other attacks in check. White-washing is also discouraged, since nodes would not want to work for the initial bootstrap score, only to abandon it and repeat the same process: it is more beneficial to preserve one's reputation through sincere cooperation. If it is more beneficial to cooperate, then peers may be discouraged from doing otherwise.

When a node misbehaves, its reputation drops, it may also be completely blacklisted depending on the type of behaviour it has exhibited. Free-riding for example may incur reputation drop naturally, while outright transmission of fake blocks would warrant blacklisting. To blacklist a node, its trust score is downgraded to -1.

Elliptical curve algorithm, namely ECDSA[3] was used for the signatures. It is preferred over other algorithms such as RSA [132] because it is faster and requires less memory and key size. We compare key lengths and key generation performance for elliptical curve cryptography (ECC) and RSA in table 6.1 [133].

Key length (bits) ECC - RSA	Key generation time(s) ECC - RSA
163 - 1024	0.08 - 0.16
233 - 2240	0.18 - 7.47
283 - 3072	0.27 - 9.80
409 - 7680	0.64 - 133.9
571 - 15360	1.44 - 679.06

Table 6.1: ECC vs RSA

- Docker and Kubernetes: As seen in earlier experiments, to test the new method, there is a need for many nodes (devices), which have to be individually loaded with necessary packages and libraries. It would be very expensive to purchase physical devices in that number, so we chose containerisation instead: Docker containers were used for this purpose. This can also be achieved using virtual machines (VM), but we chose containers because they are more economical in terms of resource consumption. For example, while containers start up within

---

[3]https://csrc.nist.gov/Projects/Elliptic-Curve-Cryptography (accessed 20/06/2019).

seconds and scale into thousands, startup time for VM is in minutes and scales in dozens. The capacity (required) for containers can also be in megabytes, while that of VM is in gigabytes; making the latter more expensive [134].

These container features make it suitable for our target use-cases, since we are focused on low-resource devices. It is lighter and makes a better match, unlike virtualization which can be a little more heavy. Nonetheless, containers can also transparently deploy tasks, just like VM. To manage the containers, kubernetes is needed. It is basically a cluster manager for Docker containers, and it is open source [135]. It is popularly used to manage heterogeneous nodes. We deployed it on a cloud-based server.

- gRPC: A multi-threaded control module was designed as part of the test bed. Since nodes are independent, we needed a way of having some control over the experimental processes. The control module is based on gRPC and enables us to remotely control each node in the network. The control mentioned here does not involve interference with the actual network protocol such as file exchange. It merely allows us to issue commands to every node at the same time, e.g. start, ping, kill, retrieve logs, etc. Among other libraries, each node runs a gRPC plugin which is used to make communication with the control module possible.

  You may ask what exactly is gRPC? It is an open source RPC (Remote Procedure Call) framework, which is known for high performance and can be deployed in any environment. It is commonly used in distributed computing to connect applications and devices to backend services [3].

6.2 Distributed Trust Ledger (DTL)

Blockchain technology emerged with promising advantages and high expectations. Among its key advantages is the ability to make transactions possible among parties that do not trust themselves; although even this arguably involves some form of trust, maybe not between nodes, but trust on the system. TRSs on the other hand focus mainly on establishing trust and security in distributed networks such as P2P, by exploring the concept of reputation.

But as we saw earlier, research is begining to be directed towards a form of convergence, where TRS is leveraged to improve trust and security in the Blockchain systems, and vice versa. The efficacy of any TRS largely depends on the security of each node's trust information/score. That is, whether or not the score is vulnerable to manipulation or false testimonies. For this reason, FBit under the FBit-U flavour employs the use of blockchain to secure the trust scores, thereby making the TRS system stronger.

Current TRSs focus mainly on managing the effect of score manipulations (e.g. bad-mouthing attacks). They apply some techniques to choose valid testimonies from a pool of received recommendations. Detected attackers may be blacklisted, but that often succeeds some damaging effect which they may have caused in the network. This section aims to exploit the immutability advantage of the Blockchain technology to eliminate the chances of bad-mouthing and similar attacks targeted at reputation scores of nodes in TRSs, and FBit in particular. A few similar reports in the literature [104, 105] are focused on different network settings and lack support for mobile edge-clouds, see section 3.4. We will discuss more about this shortly.

6.2.1 Blockchain technology

Blockchain can be viewed as a distributed ledger which is shared among its users, allowing them to perform sensitive transactions, which reflect on other ledgers, without needing an intermediary or central authority. The three basic concepts behind the technology are cryptographic algorithm, consensus mechanism and distributed ledger/database [136]. The ledger allows several parties in a network or system to add transactions to it, such that any change made consistently reflects across every copy. Because it is distributed, ledger reconciliation becomes easier, but it may require some additional computation and storage costs.

Data concerning any transaction made in the network is stored in a sequence of data blocks which are cryptographically linked. At any point in time, participants or users are able to vote on the validity of transactions and eventually agree on its sequence and system state, using a consensus mechanism. Blockchain can be permissioned or permissionless. While there is more control on the transactions that occur in a permissioned blockchain because the participants are known and easily identifiable, permissionless blockchain is more open. To prevent Sybil attack and discourage the spread of malicious contents in the open system, appending new data is made (computationally) costly.

Since its emergence in 2008 with Bitcoin [137], the technology has been applied in different sectors with the goal of gaining from its many advantages. Real estate [138], supply chain [139], finance [140], record keeping and car leasing [141] are some of the areas where Blockchain technology has been considerably featured. Although the technology can ensure immutability, it cannot guarantee the credibility of the original data/information entered into the system. This and similar other issues have prompted a debate about its "trust-less" nature, with some scholars insisting that trust remains needful in the system [142]. Accordingly, efforts have been made to introduce TRS into Blockchain as a way of further strengthening it against manipulations and attacks [101, 102].

6.2.2 Trust in Blockchain

Without trust, it would be hard to optimally reason about the security of any system [60]. It may be trust in participating peers, platform or other targets such as the products which are shared in the network. Blockchain users for example trust the system to be immutable, and the blockchain system ensures that its reputation in that context is not broken.

While the concept of trust has been heavily discussed in the context of other distributed platforms, it has received minimal attention in the context of Blockchain technology; with more focus centering on adoption, usage and business models for the technology. Blockchain is often conceived as a trust-free system, even though it remains challenging to assess whether the system is actually trust-free [136].

According to Fröwis and Böhme [143], Ethereum smart contracts do require trust because about 40 percent of such contracts do not really conform to the 'non-manipulability' status. The reports in [142, 144, 145] also upheld the need for trust in bitcoin blockchain. This has encouraged the earlier mentioned reports [101, 102] on the application of reputation and trust concepts to support blockchain.

Acknowledging the importance of trust and reputation, the strengths of blockchain can be leveraged to secure the reputation of every entity in the FBit-U system from bad-mouthing and slandering attacks. This can be viewed as the opposite of [101, 102] since it aims to take advantage of the strengths of Blockchain to safeguard TRS scores instead of the reverse (securing blockchain using TRS).

6.2.3 FBit in Blockchain

One of the key problems sabotaging the adoption of blockchain for trust management and security in distributed platforms such as mobile edge-clouds and IoT, is the huge computational resources required of each node [18], especially in proof-of-work based blockchain. It makes some sense (though not optimal) to spend sizeable amount of resources for mining in traditional crypto-currency systems such as Bitcoin, because such can be a form of investment that can yield monetary return. However, for other systems such as mobile edge-clouds [60], which may involve huge presence of (mobile) devices with low resources, a less resource intensive scheme is necessary.

Proof-of-Stake (PoS) is usually the next popular port of call, after Proof-of-Work (PoW). It also requires significant computational and memory resources for solving cryptography puzzles [146], but that can be lower compared to PoW. It can be adapted to fit into distributed networks where security, fairness and trust are needed, but at the same time, resources are meager.

Accordingly, FBit-U is further modified based on PoS, TRS and BFT (Byzantine Fault Tolerance), to establish a distributed trust ledger, such that nodes can update the behaviour of neighbours based on local and global experiences, and it would reflect on the ledger of every other peer in the network. This new method is tagged DTL (Distributed Trust Ledger). Nodes spend some "resources" to genuinely provide services to other peers at a regular rate, in order to gain priority and earn high relevance as illustrated in figure 6.1. But the resources mentioned here do not compare to that involved in PoW. We aim to exploit the properties of blockchain such as consensus, security, distributed and open access, to shield TRS scores and related information from attacks. We also plan to derive a way of storing the ledger on mobile edge-clouds, so that participating nodes can access it without keeping an entire copy locally.

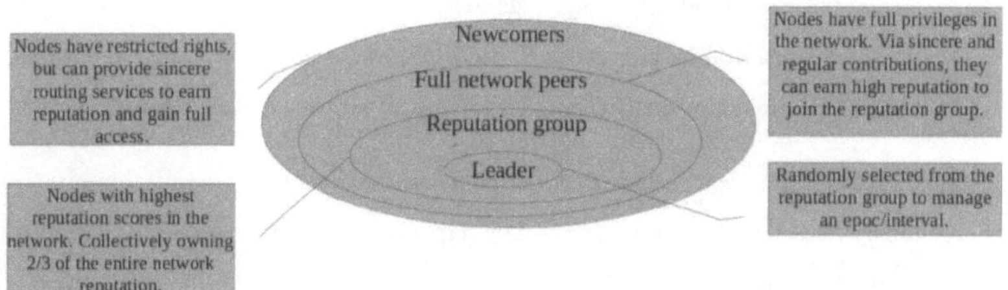

FIGURE 6.1: Precedence in DTL.

6.2.4 Reputation Bootstrapping

The DTL system is designed to be DHT compliant and would be illustrated using a Kademlia based client. It covers the four basic DHT actions which include Boostrapping, lookup, PUT and GET operations [92]. Every Kademlia participant is expected to perform a lookup, which is basically to locate k-nearest neighbours. The participant then selects α nodes from the K-neighbours and sends FIND_NODE requests to them. Each queried node returns a list of other nodes, which the initiator may further query. The entire k-bucket nodes can be queried if the α nodes fail to yield desired result. Normally, α equals three, but can vary: for example, it can be one [147].

In the proposed system, new nodes join via similar way, but the services which they can access in the network are restricted. For example they may have rights to perform lookup/routing only, while they gain reputation and qualify for full access by performing them sincerely. They can only have full rights when the bootstrap stage is completed and their reputation score is up to a certain threshold. This is consistent with FBit bootstrapping approach. Trust scores are computed locally based on individual experience, and then published on a blockchain after approval and adoption by other peers in the network, via consensus.

A newcomer would be added to the k-neighbours of the node through which it wishes to join. It can also be recommended to other nodes if the familiar node is unable to accommodate additional peer in its k-bucket at that moment. Every interaction is rated locally by the recipients. For instance, if a node returns legitimate node(s) when queried, it is counted for it as a good behaviour; while those who return malicious or non existent IDs would be denied network membership. It is also seen as a bad behaviour if a peer continuously ignores lookup requests. Similar to FBit, when responding to requests, signed packets can also be routed via newcomers, and they gain bootstrapping scores by forwarding them unadulterated. Nodes are however unable to make requests until they fulfill the bootstrap requirements and gain full access into the network.

As part of the bootstrapping process, a newcomer accumulates initial reputation by genuinely responding to routing or lookup requests. When its score fulfills the bootstrapping requirement illustrated in equation 6.3, it gets absorbed fully into the network. The process does not take long because nodes are encouraged (and actually rewarded) to admit legitimate nodes into the network. This motivates them to help newcomers by giving them opportunities to 'serve', and for each genuine service provided, their bootstrap score is calculated according to equation 6.2.

Basically, each node serviced by a newcomer computes a score locally, and then at interval, it pushes it to the blockchain. If the sum of *Bf* scores published in favour of a newcomer is up to the minimum threshold, and there is no contrary opinion, then it qualifies to be granted full access. This ensures that even a node that possesses very high capabilities and resources does not have any impact on the network at the initial stage. Similarly, continual monitoring of each node's reputation, not only slows down the time it takes for an attacker to acquire high amount of badges which gives it relevance in the network, but also helps to eliminate attackers at first (or few) malicious attempt, before it causes much harm.

Every submitted transaction contains a proof, which includes timestamp, and hash of requested and received pieces/packets, as well as the public keys of the nodes involved. Nodes generate their own key pairs before joining the network and disseminate the public keys as they transact. Newcomers do not need to service every node in the network before joining, once the *Bf* submitted by a few trusted peers confirm that they have met the minimum requirement, they will be fully admitted. That is, when $\Theta(Bf_i)$ in equation (6.3) is up to 1. This Bootstrapping technique frustrates Sybil attackers because they can only introduce a limited number, owing to lack of needed resources. It also discourages white-washing and similar other attacks because nodes would not like to loose the trust which they have laboured to build, knowing that no free score will be given if it drops to rejoin. .

$$Bf_i = \sum_c Bf_{ci}, \tag{6.2}$$

$$\Theta(Bf_i) = \begin{cases} 0 & \text{if Bf} < n_{min} \\ 1 & \text{otherwise} \end{cases}, \tag{6.3}$$

where Bf_i is the Bootstrap factor credited to the new node_i, according to the bootstrap factors published by other nodes_c concerning node_i. The final bootstrapping outcome ($\Theta(Bf)$) can either be 0 or 1, as illustrated in equation (6.3). n_{min} is the Bf threshold. Notice that there is no longer the need to collect recommended bootstrap factors as was done in FBit.

In general, nodes at intervals publish scores of top nodes and newcomers (if any), based on their local experience within that interval. Other nodes queue behind the scores they agree with, or initiate another branch if they disagree. At the end of the interval, a leader compiles valid transactions into block(s), and adds it to the blockchain, similar to [102]. Valid votes need to have a minimum amount of resources (we call this badges) staked in its favour, and like in Bitcoin, the heaviest branch wins, if multiple exist. Existing nodes go through the same process while publishing newcomers' scores. More explanation regarding the score publication procedure shall be given subsequently.

When a peer suspects any act of maliciousness (e.g. an existing node trying to introduce a nonexistent newcomer), it can ask for evidence of the transaction from the node who submitted it, and such can be published against the malicious node. If the node refuses to reply; that too can be published as an evidence against it. The evidence is analyzed, and if the node is considered malicious, it will be blacklisted. The process of evidence analysis is similar to other transactions; a node can flag a suspected malicious agent, providing some proof, while other nodes either agree or disagree. Like in BitcoinNG [148] a leader is elected at the beginning of intervals and it moderates transactions until a new one is elected.

The use of puzzle [83] could be an alternative method of bootstrapping, but it is only a test of resources, not a test of reputation. This means that a node with much resources will be able to attack the network to the tune of its resources, as soon as it joins. But our method of bootstrapping tests for both resources and reputation, meaning that a node with same amount of resource will take longer time to introduce sybils which would be used to attack the network. Also, the attacker is likely going to be detected and eliminated before completing the bootstrap process since reputation check begins at the initial attempt to join. Moreover, the resources used during the bootstrapping process are at the same time utilized to send valuable packets, unlike the puzzle method which only serves one purpose.

6.2.5 Familiarity

Each node keeps track of how frequent other peers interact or respond to its requests. This is used to know how much each neighbour has contributed to the local node in particular, and to the entire network by extension. As previously mentioned, it is different from reputation which is a reflection of how genuine the interactions/contributions were. The equation used for this is same as (4.3).

6.2.6 Reputation computation

To keep track of the direct reputation that accompany the interaction rate of each node, the probability expectation value of beta distribution [33] is applied to compute local reputation. α represents the number of genuine transactions, while β captures the number of malicious transactions and number of uploads (that was in favor of the node being accessed). This among other things, helps a trustor to know how much it has given to the trustee compared to how much it has received from it; reflecting a kind of tit-for-tat attribute. The bootstrapping factor also comes into play here, and equation (4.4) is re-used to compute the direct reputation experience.

6.2.7 System description (Post Bootstrapping)

After the bootstrapping process and local trust computation, nodes propose trust updates at intervals, regarding the top performing nodes in their local list. This is done by proposing that the trustee's reputation score be updated to reflect its recent performance. Other nodes who have also interacted with that trustee will then vote in support, or against - if they feel that the current proposal does not reflect their local experience. A leader manages an epoc, including overseeing the votes.

In case of multiple endorsement chains, the heaviest branch is adopted; in-terms of length, badges and reputation, as illustrated in figure (6.2). That is; $\sum_{v=1}^{n} GS_v * \sum SB$, where v stands for nodes that have endorsed a given transaction, GS_v is the trust score of each v, and SB represents the staked badges. Nodes can vote, endorse or propose a counter score even if their experience was not gained within the current interval: it must however not be based on a very old interval. Moreover, they need to have transaction evidence to support their claims. Other forms of proposal (e.g. transactions) are also done in a similar manner.

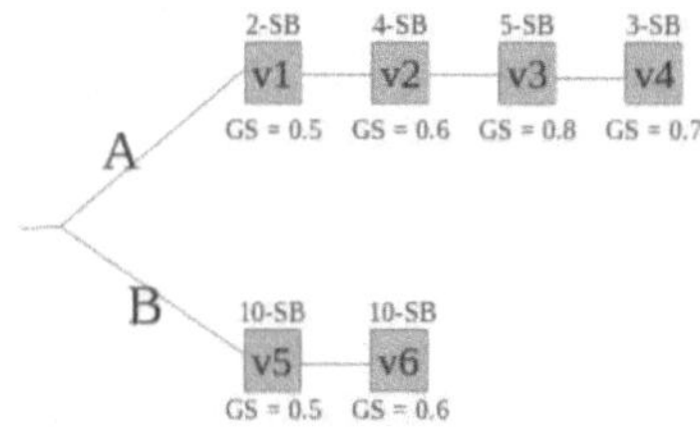

FIGURE 6.2: Resolving a fork in an endorsement chain

Figure (6.2) illustrates a disagreement in an endorsement chain; it could be a proposal for score update, or compiled block made up of trust scores which needs to be added to the main blockchain. In this example, chain B would have been adopted if it were only based on resources possessed, since $v5$ and $v6$ staked many more badges. But in addition to other blockchain attributes, DTL further considers trust : *"A"* would therefore be rightfully adopted. The minimum stake required for a given type of proposal/endorsement may vary, e.g proposal for score update may require less SB, while proposal/endorsement of a block may require higher staked-batches. But the method of fork resolution remains similar.

When the proposal of any node is adopted, the node is rewarded with some badge units, if the transaction is not reported as malicious for a number of preceding intervals. Nodes that have voted to support the proposal also share in the badge reward, as well as the leader that commits the block to blockchain. Greater percentage of the reward goes to the leader, followed by the initiator of the proposal, and the least goes to the nodes who have voted in support. This is basically how nodes accumulate badges. The initial badge unit is assigned to the node after gaining "high" reputation. The value of 'high reputation' can be set as desired, paying attention to the network needs.

If on the other hand the transaction is reported to be malicious within the probation period, then the leader and the initiator would be punished. The probation period of a block ends the moment another block is committed. Verification which is usually done by the reputation group, can be done alongside 'mining' of the next block, to save time.

The more badges a node has, the more influence it has in the network. A node needs to stake some badge(s) when making or supporting any proposal. The stakes can be lost if the added node or transaction is reported and confirmed malicious, otherwise it appreciates. When choosing the reputation group, badges are considered alongside reputation scores.

The reputation group consists of y number of nodes with top trust scores: they are dynamically chosen and need to communally possess a given percentage of the entire reputation/trust score in the network (e.g. 2/3). Each member of the group is also required to possess a minimum fraction of badge units, relative to the total badges in the network. Since the trust and badge information is publicly available, if the duration of each epoch (in time or number of nodes) is also known (synchronous), it would be easy to agree on election/re-election of leaders and consensus group members.

If the system is asynchronous, then timing is done by consensus also: any node can initiate an end-of-tenure vote regarding the current leader/miner, based on number of committed blocks, or suspicion of maliciousness according to local experience. The vote can be endorsed by other peers, and a new leader would be chosen. This can be coordinated by a randomly selected node from the reputation group or volunteer from the group.

6.2.7.1 Miner election

Our work builds on the principles of [102, 148], with needful adjustments. Time is divided into epochs, and a leader is selected to manage each epoch; the leader is expected to process up to n number of blocks within an epoch. n can be derived from the average number of blocks that leaders are able to commit within an interval.

Leaders who commit significantly less number may raise suspicion, since such act may frustrate the network if a malicious leader is elected by chance. In the new method, nodes gain reputation and badges as rewards for consistency and sincere contribution to the network. Newcomers are allowed to join partially until they prove reliable. They qualify for initial badge units after gaining "high" reputation, and from then, they move on to become miners/leaders if they act consistently. It is important to note that DTL only complements FBit-U, which means that most transactions still happen in a similar way, while blockchain is adopted for better security and publicity.

As already noted, to propose (or support) any score update or transaction for public adoption, nodes need to stake some badge units. If the proposed (or supported) transaction is adopted and sustained as valid, the staked badges appreciate, otherwise they would be lost. The system rewards 'miners' whose proposals are adopted, with additional badge units. The reward is shared among contributors to that proposal: the initiator, voters/endorsers, and leader who commits the block. The reward is added to the staked badges and credited back to its owners. Nothing is added if the endorsed proposal is not generally accepted. To select a miner therefore, a node is randomly selected from the reputation group.

When the current epoch is about to expire, any node within the reputation group may initiate a random selection process for selecting a new leader, while other group members either support the selection or initiate another if they disagree. The process is similar to other forms of transaction; badges need to be staked, which may be rewarded or lost. Heaviest branch always wins, and the node in that branch becomes the new leader; it announces itself through a broadcast, attaching its vote and public key information. When a leader becomes quiet or inefficient (in-terms of honesty and speed), any other node in the group can initiate a process to elect another leader.

The agreement procedure used in this work fundamentally follows Byzantine fault tolerance (BFT) protocols, which require a minimum of two-third (2/3) genuine nodes to keep the network protected from attackers [102]. To strengthen this further, the proposed system further requires that voters of adopted blocks need to collectively possess a reputation score which is up to a given threshold, e.g. 1/3 of total reputation.

In the new system, nodes stake a given number of badges to vote or initiate a proposal, while the reputation of the voters further define the weight of each vote, ensuring that resources and reputation jointly play a role in the consensus process. More reputable nodes have better chances of getting services, and having their services accepted, which advances the influence of the node in the network.

The system can dynamically determine the minimum stake required for transactions in the network, based on availability (or otherwise) of badge units. Initiators of the network generate the genesis block, and since each block contains evidence of transactions, nodes that join subsequently can verify its validity.

Because everyone can see the scores and proves of transactions surrounding each score, the risk of badmouthing or slandering attacks [18] is minimal or nonexistent. Furthermore, because it takes badges to propose or support a proposal, Sybil attack is also very minimal; considering the fact that badges are gained with a combination of resources (spent while working for it) and accumulated sincerity (earned by not acting maliciously over time). Nodes who propose fake/malicious peers will have their badges revoked, and they would lose their relevance. Other forms of attacks such as fake-block and bandwidth attacks are addressed by reputation (DT) and interaction rate (IR) computations respectively.

6.3 Summary

The processes that can be followed to adapt the proposed system to blockchain have been outlined. Since PoW is not feasible in our kind of network, we have proposed a modified PoS system that does not involve heavy resources. A number of reports have suggested the use of TRS to improve trust in blockchian, but we have focused on the reverse - applying the blockchain concepts to secure trust scores, in a way that can accommodate mobile devices and other low capacity nodes. This part of the work is not completed yet; it is still theoretical, yet to be tested.

The generated stakes as well as the reputation of each node serve as the transaction coin, it can be re-used in the network when a node leaves to join at a later time. Although FBit and its variants are robust and effective as they are now, deploying it to blockchain as proposed here would extend their use cases tremendously. Blockchain attributes such as immutability and public access would be inherited by the new system. However, we envisage scalability issues, like the case is with many Blockchain applications. FBit-U which is a variant of FBit, aimed at functioning in a containerized platform, was introduced alongside its test-bed; it featured a DHT protocol, Docker and Kubernetes. In practice, FBit-U is a subset of DTL, not a different project.

Chapter 7

Conclusion

Computing is becoming increasingly distributed, especially with the advent of edge computing, IoT and related technologies. To maintain improved quality of service (QoS) and user experience in IoT applications, nodes need to rely less on central agents (such as the cloud) for computation and data handling. Edge computing paradigms are used to achieve this. These paradigms offer many advantages, but there are also some security implications, and solutions need to evolve at a similar pace which the technologies emerge.

The literature has documented TRS as optimal for addressing the security needs of distributed networks. Their real life applications have been more in semi distributed systems such as eBay, Yahoo, Amazon, and in some others such as Kazaa. However, there are issues that remain unsolved in these systems which limit their efficacy in the present setups, and (more importantly) limit their application in the mentioned emerging technologies. Such issues were identified and addressed in this book.

One of the major issues identified and resolved is a loophole that can lead to bandwidth attack, which remained unaddressed prior to our work, especially in distributed P2P and related protocols including mobile edge-clouds. A P2P system is usually a give-and-take platform, which means that every node can act as a client and as a server. If it is a file sharing platform, every node downloads and uploads to others from the portion it already has. There are nodes who start as seeders and others who become seeders by completing their downloads/transactions, and then staying back to help other nodes. The server nodes (seeders) are often fooled by malicious client nodes who take advantage of the fact that they lack firsthand information about the upload behaviour of other nodes at recent intervals, leading to bandwidth attack.

Another identified loophole has to do with kick-starting newcomers' reputations via default scores or other heuristics that do not reflect their actual behaviours. This is contrary to the basic trust requirements as already pointed out, and could encourage white-washing or related malicious acts. It was addressed using our bootstrapping technique which assigns scores that correspond to the node's actual behaviour. This helped to minimise Sybil attack and makes white-washing less appealing.

Also among the considered weaknesses of the existing systems is the fact that they do not adequately account for the concept of familiarity. A cooperative node should be rewarded not just for not attacking the network but also for being a consistent contributor. It is also not enough to just cancel out a node's number of downloads with its number of uploads. The problem with this method is that if a node downloads two pieces for example, and uploads two pieces also, then it may be considered the same as another node who has upload 500 pieces and equally downloaded 500 pieces. As explained earlier in this work, our view is that trust scores need to better capture 'contribution' not just 'non-maliciousness' - this would encourage better participation.

The TRSs used in systems like eBay and Amazon have some form of centralization, which makes them more coordinated. But in more distributed platforms, handling reputations and recommendations can be more problematic. Our system introduces a way of maintaining distributed 'registration' and preliminary screening via bootstrapping, as well as a form of access control - since nodes can have privileges that correspond to their reputations and commitments to the network (badges).

Peersim simulator which is an event driven simulator for P2P was used for the testbed. Modified BitTorrent (which is one of the most popular P2P protocol) was used for the simulations. This allowed us to establish the behaviour of the algorithm in a known protocol, prior to modifications to reflect the attributes of the newer protocols, namely mobile edge-clouds. The proposed system was also tested on a simulated IoT based eHealth system, which is one of the possible use cases of mobile edge-clouds. Results from both experiments show the robustness and scalability of the proposed method.

www.ingramcontent.com/pod-product-compliance
Lightning Source LLC
LaVergne TN
LVHW041721190726
843493LV00007B/2190